# The Nonverbal Communication Workbook

# The Nonverbal Communication Workbook

## Joseph A. DeVito
*Hunter College of the City University of New York*

WAVELAND
PRESS, INC.
Prospect Heights, Illinois

For information about this book, write or call:

Waveland Press, Inc.
P.O. Box 400
Prospect Heights, Illinois 60070
(847) 634-0081

**Consulting Editors**

Joseph A. DeVito
Robert E. Denton, Jr.

# Table of Contents

# 2 Body Communication . . . . . . . . . . . . . . . . . . . . . 37

# 3 Facial and Eye Communication . . . . . . . 63

# 4 Artifactual Communication ............. 81

# 5 Spatial Communication (Proxemics and Territoriality) ............... 109

# 6  Tactile Communication (Haptics) ...... 135

# Appendix A
## Some Applications to Interpersonal Communication . . . . . . 241

# Appendix B
## Researching Nonverbal Communication . . . . . . . . . . . . . . . . . 265

## Readings in Nonverbal Communication . . . . . . . . . . . . . . . . . . . . . 281

# Acknowledgments

It is a pleasure to thank the many people who have contributed to this workbook. When I first began teaching nonverbal communication, many of my colleagues shared their knowledge and insights with me. I especially wish to thank Pat Stack of Nassau Community College, Enid Portnoy and Virginia Richmond of West Virginia University, Helen Newman of Hunter College, and Michael Hecht of Arizona State University. Much of what is good in this workbook is due to these people although they are not responsible for what may not be so good. The workbooks of Virginia Richmond and Steven Payne (*Nonverbal Communication: A Workbook and Study Guide*), John Trombetta (*Workbook for Nonverbal Communication*), Barry Morganstern, Enid Portnoy, and Peter Andersen (*Communicating Nonverbally: A Workbook and Study Guide for Nonverbal Communication*), and Don Stacks (*Exploring Nonverbal Communication: A Workbook to Accompany "NVC Nonverbal Communication*) were most helpful in clarifying the role of a workbook in the nonverbal communication course.

I also owe a debt of thanks to those who allowed their materials to be used here; I have included references to these people throughout the text.

Last, I thank Carol and Neil Rowe of Waveland Press for making this text a pleasure to write and produce.

# Preface

The *Nonverbal Communication Workbook* is designed to be used in the introductory course in nonverbal communication and may be used as the primary text or in conjunction with any of several textbooks, books of readings, or popular books on nonverbal communication. Its functions are three-fold:

1. to provide overviews of the various areas of nonverbal communication;

2. to provide exercises that will promote active learning of the concepts and principles discussed in the text and in class lectures-discussions; and

3. to provide materials to guide the further study and review of the material covered in this nonverbal communication course.

The *Workbook* consists of ten chapters and two appendixes. Chapter One provides some beginning perspectives for the study of nonverbal communication, identifies the major areas of nonverbal communication, and introduces some of the major terms current in the field. Chapters Two through Ten cover the standard topics in nonverbal communication: (2) *body communication* (how body type communicates and how body movements and gestures communicate); (3) *facial and eye communication* (how facial expressions and eye movements communicate); (4) *artifactual communication* (how objects, clothing, jewelry, furnishings, colors, and other adornments communicate); (5) *spatial communication* (how use of space in interpersonal interactions and how the layout of homes and offices communicate as well as ownership-like reactions to different areas of space, marking of such spaces, and defense of these areas); (6) *tactile communication* (how we communicate through touch); (7) *para-language and silence* (how the rate, volume, quality, pauses and hesitations, and pitch communicate and the varied meanings that silence can communicate); (8) *smell* (how scent is used to communicate a wide variety of messages); (9) *temporal communication* (how our use of time communicates); and (10) *deception and deception detection* (how we lie and detect the lies of others through nonverbal means).

Each chapter opens with an overview of the area of nonverbal communication. These overviews will prove most effective if they are supplemented by additional readings and/or lectures-discussions. The second part of each chapter contains exercises designed to provide hands-on experience with the various dimensions of nonverbal communication. There are a total of 75 exercises in this workbook. Obviously not all of these can be considered in any given course. However, the menu of choices is sufficiently large and varied so that the needs and purposes of most courses may be met. Where relevant, space has been provided to record reactions, questions, and answers. These exercises will prove most beneficial when done in conjunction with extensive reading in the specific area of nonverbal communication.

Learning a new academic discipline is largely, though by no means limited to, the learning of a specialized vocabulary. Therefore, included in each chapter is a list of terms essential to the understanding of nonverbal communication. Space has been provided to record the definitions and pertinent examples. Space is also provided to record any additional terms and definitions that are used in the conduct of the course.

Appendix A contains a variety of exercises designed to illustrate some of the varied applications that can be made of nonverbal communication to interpersonal communication generally. These exercises may be considered together and used as a final unit to the course or may be integrated throughout the course. These exercises are especially useful for bringing together the various aspects of nonverbal communication. Rather than focusing on the specific modality of communication (for example, whether touch or time or space), these exercises focus on interpersonal issues such as conflict, dating, and drawing inferences from nonverbal messages. Thus, the exercises in Appendix A bring together *all* the ways in which nonverbal messages may be communicated.

Appendix B, Researching Nonverbal Communication, is included as a guide to the design and execution of an original experiment in nonverbal communication, a common class project. In this appendix are included four preliminary exercises ("Abstracting a Research Study," "Formulating Hypotheses," "Defining Nonverbal Variables Operationally," and "Evaluating 'Research' Claims") designed to raise some initial issues and to introduce the research process. The rather detailed "Designing and Conducting A Research Project in Nonverbal Communication" provides suggestions for conducting a research study and a format for writing up the study.

The Workbook should serve as a record of progress through this exciting but often confusing area of communication. The definitions of the field combined with personal thoughts, reactions, and experiences relevant to the wide variety of nonverbal communication issues introduced should make the exploration of nonverbal communication a valuable, *shared* experience.

A rather extensive bibliography of nonverbal communication concludes this workbook. This should prove helpful in selecting articles to abstract (one of the exercises in Appendix B), to pursue further reading, and to provide useful source material for the nonverbal research project.

An instructor's manual is available from Waveland Press. This manual keys the workbook to a number of different texts and also provides guidelines for using the various exercises.

# Approaching the Study of Nonverbal Communication

## Ten Suggestions

Nonverbal communication is one of the most interesting areas of study that you will encounter in your college career. It is also, however, very different from other academic areas and needs to be approached with some specific guidelines in mind. Here are ten suggestions for guiding your study of this new and exciting area of nonverbal communication so that you may be able to derive the greatest benefits.

1. Self-analysis is essential if you are to use this material in any meaningful sense, for example, to change some of your own behaviors. Be honest with yourself about your virtues as well as your vices, your satisfactions and dissatisfactions.

2. Observe. Observe. Observe. Observe the behaviors of those around you as well as your own. See in everyday behavior what you read about here and discuss in class.

3. Never draw conclusions from isolated bits of nonverbal behaviors. Nonverbal communication occurs in packages of movements and gestures and these packages of behaviors are greatly influenced by the entire communication context as well as by the verbal communications they accompany. Look at the entire package. See the forest as well as the individual trees.

4. Resist the temptation to draw conclusions from just nonverbal behaviors. In fact, never draw conclusions on the basis of nonverbal behaviors alone. Instead, formulate hypotheses (educated guesses) about what motivates the behaviors or what the effects of such-and-such behaviors might be and, most important, be prepared to prove yourself wrong.

5. Postpone attempts to apply this new knowledge until you have examined the whole of nonverbal communication. Especially resist giving others advice on their nonverbal behaviors. Applications on the basis of too little information are usually incorrect and often dangerous.

6.  Read widely. Begin a personal library on nonverbal communication. This is an area of study you're not going to forget once the course ends. You will always and everywhere be communicating nonverbally and using the insights learned here. Save the articles in newspapers, magazines, professional journals, textbooks, and popular books that you use in this course or come across in your readings. Numerous suggestions for additional reading are provided throughout this *Workbook*.

7.  Connect and relate. Although the areas of nonverbal communication are presented separately in textbooks, in actual communication situations, they all work together. Part of the task in learning nonverbal communication is to draw the relevant connections among the different areas so that you end up with a complete (or relatively complete) picture of the communication act.

8.  Realize that the results of research and the conclusions presented here, in your other readings, and in lectures and discussions are true in a statistical sense. They apply to the average or typical person and may or may not apply to you, to your family members, or to your friends as individuals.

9.  Learn to appreciate differences in nonverbal communication much as you would appreciate differences in colors or flowers or foods. Yet, also recognize that conformity to a standard, say in dress or in following rules of etiquette, may be a requisite for being hired or promoted.

10. Learn the new vocabulary of nonverbal communication and begin to think with this new vocabulary. Make the technical language of nonverbal communication part of your active vocabulary. The new terms will help you to highlight and to focus on what might normally pass undetected.

# 1

# Beginning Perspectives

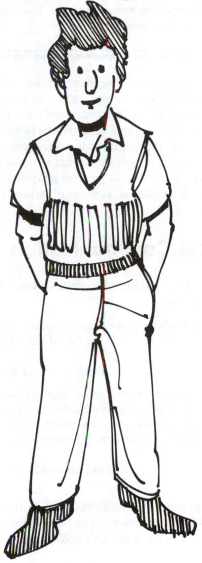

## Chapter Outline

The Definition of Nonverbal
   Communication
The Areas of Nonverbal
   Communication
Intentionality and Nonintentionality
The Functions of Nonverbal
   Communication
The Characteristics of Nonverbal
   Communication
   *Communicative*
   *Contextual*
   *Believable*
   *Rule-Governed*
   *Metacommunicational*
   *Packaged*

## Objectives

After completing this chapter, you should be able to:

1. define *nonverbal communication*
2. identify and define at least eight areas or subdivisions of nonverbal communication
3. explain the role of intentionality and nonintentionality in communication and especially in nonverbal communication
4. identify the six functions of nonverbal communication and give examples of each
5. explain the communicative, contextual, believable, rule-governed, metacommunicational, and packaged nature of nonverbal communication

In this chapter we present some beginning perspectives, some ways of looking at and defining nonverbal communication in broad terms. We present these beginning perspectives by looking at (1) the definition of nonverbal communication, (2) the areas of nonverbal communication, (3) the functions that nonverbal communication serves, and (4) some general characteristics or qualities of nonverbal communication. These discussions will serve as a foundation for later chapters in which we go into the specific areas of nonverbal communication in greater detail.

# The Definition of Nonverbal Communication

Nonverbal communication may be defined in various ways. Here are a few definitions to get us started:

> the process of (an) individual(s) transmitting nonverbal cues that have the potential to stimulate meaning in the mind(s) of (an) other individual(s)
>
> Malandro and Barker, p. 9

> those attributes or actions of humans, other than the use of words themselves, which have socially shared meanings, are intentionally sent or interpreted as intentional, are consciously sent or consciously received, and have the potential for feedback from the receiver
>
> Burgoon and Saine, pp. 9-10

> the process of one person stimulating meaning in the mind of another person (or persons) by meanings of nonverbal messages
>
> Richmond, McCroskey, and Payne, p. 1

A much simpler way to define nonverbal communication is to say that it is communication without words. Note that we say that nonverbal communication is *without words*, **not** *without sound*. Pitch, rate, and volume, for example, are nonverbal communication dimensions because they do not involve words.

# The Areas of Nonverbal Communication

We may also define nonverbal communication by identifying the several areas that comprise nonverbal communication. In this view, then, nonverbal communication would consist of those messages that are sent and received through these "nonverbal channels." Here are several areas most often included in the study of nonverbal communication:

1. *Body communication:* how our body type communicates impressions concerning our personality and general behavior patterns and how our gestures and gross body movements communicate.
2. *Facial communication:* how our facial movements communicate meanings.
3. *Eye Communication:* how we communicate through the type and length of eye contact and eye avoidance and how the dilation and constriction of pupils communicate different meanings.
4. *Artifactual communication:* how clothing, hair style, jewelry, home furnishings, office decoration, and colors communicate.
5. *Spatial communication (proxemics):* how our use of space in our interpersonal interactions and in the arrangement of our homes and offices communicate.
6. *Territoriality:* how our ownership-like reactions to areas of space influence our behaviors, how we may encroach upon the territory of others, and how we may react to such encroachments.
7. *Tactile communication (haptics):* how we communicate by touch.
8. *Paralanguage:* how we communicate through changes in rate, volume, quality, resonance, pitch, and pauses and hesitations and the impressions that we formulate on the basis of these variations.

9. **Silence:** the absence of speech and the meanings that may be communicated by silence.
10. **Smell (olfactics):** how we communicate through odor and the messages we derive from different smells.
11. **Temporal communication (chronemics):** how our use of time communicates and how our time preferences and biological clocks may influence other behaviors.

## Intentionality and Nonintentionality

Over 100 years ago R. Kleinpaul, in *Sprache ohne Worte*, noted that nonverbal behavior may be classified into three main categories: with intention and with communication; with intention but without communication; and without intention and without communication. We might also add a fourth possibility: without intention and with communication. Taking all four possibilities we may arrange these into the following matrix:

|  | With Intention | Without Intention |
|---|---|---|
| With Communication | 1 | 2 |
| Without Communication | 3 | 4 |

Here we have the four possibilities for intentionality and communication. Note that in Square 1, we have what we normally think of as communication: we intend to communicate certain messages and we do in fact achieve this end; our messages are received. In Square 2 we have no intention of communicating but we do nevertheless. This type of communication occurs frequently. We want to appear calm and in control but our palms sweat, our legs shake, and our speech contains frequent and overly-long pauses; we thus communicate our nervousness and our discomfort without any intention of doing so.

In Square 3 we intend to communicate but for one or more reasons we fail to achieve communication; perhaps we say the wrong thing or perhaps the other person simply doesn't hear. On a somewhat more sophisticated level, consider the situation in which we try to tell another person something. If that person is preoccupied with other issues or detached due to some psychological barrier, he or she might fail to receive our message as we intended it to be received. In Square 4 we have the situation in which we have no intention to communicate and we do not in fact communicate. An obvious example of this might occur when we behave in a certain way without intending to communicate and no one notices. We have behaved but have not been observed and so our signals are not received.

Although not all researchers are in agreement as to which of these situations can legitimately be called communication, my own feeling is that Squares 1, 2, and 3 represent communication—or, in our case, nonverbal communication—but that Square 4 is simply behavior without communication. Note that Square 4 includes behaviors that are not observed by another person; these are not behaviors that we would consider occurring in an interactional situation. All behaviors occurring in an interactional situation, as explained below under the "communicative" quality of nonverbal communication, are communication.

This distinction between intention and unintentional behavior is particularly interesting because it brings into focus the important principle that we communicate whether we intend to or not. Further, when we realize the broad range of nonverbal signals with which we are dealing, it should be clear that our nonverbal messages are inevitable. For example, we communicate by the clothes we wear, whether or not it was our intention to communicate. As will be seen throughout this text and this course, our communications stand a much greater chance of achieving their goal when they are intentional and when we are aware of their potential for creating meanings in the minds of others.

# The Functions of Nonverbal Communication

Nonverbal communication—as can be appreciated from the above list of areas—is extremely broad and, not surprisingly, extremely powerful as a means of communication. We can use nonverbal messages to serve a variety of functions. Here we single out six major functions of nonverbal communication, following the lead of nonverbal researchers Paul Ekman, Mark Knapp, and others.

1. *to accent:* to highlight, to stress, to emphasize some part of the verbal message, for example, to speak a key word at a high volume or to open our eyes especially wide while asking a question

2. *to complement:* to complete, to supplement, to add to the verbal message, for example, to speak of hatred with clenched teeth and a tense and serious body posture

3. *to contradict:* to communicate messages nonverbally that are opposite to the verbal messages, for example, to say ''I love you'' while avoiding eye contact or to say ''I'm really interested in what you're saying'' while yawning

4. *to regulate:* to control, to coordinate the flow of verbal messages, for example, to purse your lips and move your head toward the speaker when you wish to say something or to shake your head in approval to indicate to the speaker that you wish to hear more

5. *to repeat:* to restate, to reinforce the verbal messages, for example, to point a finger at someone while saying ''he's the one'' or to make the O.K. sign with our fingers while saying ''okay''

6. *to substitute:* to take the place of a verbal message, for example, nodding your head instead of verbalizing ''yes'' or waving goodbye instead of saying anything

# The Characteristics of Nonverbal Communication

One last approach to explaining and defining nonverbal communication is to identify those characteristics that are common to all (or most) areas of nonverbal communication and to all (or most) nonverbal messages. Here we single out six major characteristics. Nonverbal behaviors are communicative, contextual, believable, rule-governed, metacommunicational (frequently), and packaged (often).

## Communicative

Nonverbal behaviors, in an interactional situation, just like verbal behaviors, always communicate. Sometimes these messages are obvious as when we wave goodbye or give someone a "thumbs up" sign. Sometimes, however, these messages are extremely subtle as, for example, when we communicate our attraction for another person by maintaining prolonged eye contact, by the enlargement of our pupils, or by imitating that other person's nonverbal behaviors.

## Contextual

Nonverbal communication always takes place in a context. Beware of drawing inferences solely from one bit of nonverbal behavior without taking into consideration the entire verbal and nonverbal context of which it is a part. The meaning of any given bit of nonverbal behavior can only be determined by examining the context in which the behavior takes place. A raised hand in a classroom, for example, may communicate a desire to speak. At an auction, this same behavior might communicate a desire to purchase a product or signal a bid. At a parliamentary meeting it may signal a vote of approval. In short, the context is always a part of the meaning communicated by nonverbal behaviors.

## Believable

One of the most publicized facts about nonverbal communication is that it is highly believable. When, for example, verbal and nonverbal messages contradict each other, we generally tend to believe the nonverbal. Furthermore, we tend to look for the meanings behind nonverbal behaviors when we have any reason to doubt the truthfulness of the speaker. One researcher, for example, has proposed that *in the communication of feelings* the relative importance of the communication channels is represented in the following formula:

**Total impact of the message = .07 verbal + .38 vocal + .55 facial**

In this formula 93% of the total impact is due to nonverbal messages.

Most researchers, however, would be more conservative and would hold that approximately 60 to 65 percent of a message's impact is due to nonverbal factors.

The exact percentages will, of course, vary from one communication situation to another and so the specific percentages are not especially important. What is important to note, however, is that a significant portion of our communications consist of nonverbal message elements, and if we are to control our communications effectively and to understand the communications of others, we have to devote considerable attention to the nonverbal dimension of communication.

## Rule-Governed

Nonverbal communication is rule-governed. Our culture dictates that certain forms of nonverbal communication are appropriate (for example, holding the arm of a person in need of help getting into a cab) and certain forms are inappropriate (for example, holding the arm of a stranger we see on the street). Some forms are acceptable in certain contexts (screaming at a football game) and unacceptable in other contexts (screaming in a college classroom). In many of the exercises in this *Workbook* the rule-governed nature of nonverbal communication is emphasized and explored.

## Metacommunicational

Language is most frequently used to refer to the world of objects, people, and events. We sometimes refer to this as "object communication." However, language may also be used to talk about language itself, and when it does, we refer to it as *metalanguage*. Statements such as "That statement was difficult to understand" or "How do you say 'goodbye' in Spanish?" are metalinguistic or metalanguage statements because they refer to language rather than to some object, event, or person in the outside world. In a similar way, when we talk about communication, we may refer to such talk as *metacommunicational*.

Nonverbal communication may also refer to the world of objects, events, and people and be "object communication." For example, when we point or smile or nod our heads we are generally referring to something outside the world of language and these would clearly be examples of object communication. But nonverbal communication messages may also—and very frequently do—comment on other messages (verbal or nonverbal), for example, the smile when we expresspleasure at meeting someone and the clenched teeth when we glare at someone we dislike. When nonverbal messages comment on other messages, we refer to them as metacommunicational.

And so, although both verbal and nonverbal messages may serve a metacommunicational function, we emphasize this role with nonverbal messages because they so frequently serve this function. If you review the six functions of nonverbal communication considered above, you will note the frequency of this metacommunicational function.

## Packaged

Nonverbal messages are best viewed in terms of "packages" or as a collection of signals all communicating essentially the same meaning. When, for example, we are happy to see someone and greet them, we communicate this feeling with our body posture, our eyes, our facial expression, and our handshake, at the very least. Similarly, when we express fear we do so with our entire body—with our eyes, our facial expressions, and our body posture.

When we attempt to look for meaning in nonverbal communication, therefore, we must examine the entire range of nonverbal behaviors and not focus on just the eyes or just the facial expressions. When we fail to do this—and try to read meaning into one specific nonverbal behavior—we will invariably miss a great deal. The more nonverbal behaviors we take into consideration, the greater are our chances of drawing correct inferences.

Usually, these packages of messages are consistent. The eyes, the facial expressions, and the body posture all communicate the same meanings. In these situations, we seldom bring the nonverbal messages to consciousness. They seem so natural that we don't think about them. When, however, these packages contain inconsistencies—when there is a smile that says "I'm pleased to see you" but a lack of eye contact that says "I'm not pleased to see you"—we perk up and notice that something is wrong and then focus on the specific nonverbal behaviors. When confronted with such inconsistencies, we may conclude that there is some conflict in the feelings of the person or perhaps that there is some deception going on. Regardless of what conclusion we come to, and regardless of whether our conclusions are right or wrong, the point to note is that inconsistent packages draw attention to themselves and probably merit some investigation.

# Beginning Perspectives Exercises

The *Workbook* exercises in this first chapter are designed to enable you to explore the area of nonverbal communication and to obtain a first glimpse into the range and depth of this area of study. These goals are addressed in *An Introductory Quiz in Nonverbal Communication* and *The Areas of Nonverbal Communication*. The nature of nonverbal communication is further explored through contrasting it with our more familiar verbal system or language in *Verbal and Nonverbal Message Systems* and through analyzing its several functions in *The Functions of Nonverbal Communication*.

The rule-governed nature of nonverbal communication is introduced in *Rule-Keeping and Rule-Breaking*. This rule-governed nature is a theme to which we return throughout this workbook. In *Giving Instructions Nonverbally* we try to illustrate in broad outline the various types of nonverbal messages we have at our disposal. In *Approaches to Nonverbal Communication* we encourage you to inquire into the point of view of your text(s). The first exercise, *First Impressions*, is designed to enable class members to interact and to get to know each other. Further, it should illustrate a number of important general principles of nonverbal communication.

# 1.1  Forming First Impressions*

This exercise is designed to raise a variety of issues concerning first impressions. Two specific aims are to sensitize you to the wide range of cues you give off to others and receive from others and to analyze the basis on which first impressions are formed.

The general procedure is as follows: break up into dyads with someone to whom you have not previously spoken. That is, you should form a dyad with a total stranger. For five minutes discuss one of the following topics: television, sports, or education. Do **not** read any further until you have completed these five minute discussions.

After the discussion, respond as specifically and as accurately as possible to the following questions about the person with whom you have just interacted.

**Identifying data:**

1. Name_____

2. Age_____

3. Occupation and/or college major_____

4. Relational status_____

5. Political orientation (liberal, conservative, democratic, republican, active, passive, ?)

_____

6. Music preferences (rock, disco, jazz, popular, classical, country/western, etc.)

_____

**Cues used in guessing identifying data:** [For example, clothing, jewelry, hair style, facial expressions, eye behavior, spatial relationships maintained, sitting posture, vocal characteristics (rate, pitch, volume, quality), touching behavior, gestures, etc.]

_____

_____

_____

**Some Attitudes:**

Using the scale presented below, indicate the extent to which you think the person with whom you just interacted agrees or disagrees with each of the following propositions:

        1 = strongly agrees
        2 = agrees
        3 = is relatively neutral
        4 = disagrees
        5 = strongly disagrees

1. The legalization of marijuana: _____

2. Gay and lesbian rights bills: _____

3. Manditory retirement at age 65: _____

4. Setting the legal drinking age at 21: _____

5. The Equal Rights Amendment (ERA): _____

**Cues used in guessing attitudes:** _____

_____

_____

**Interpersonal Communication Patterns:**

Respond to the following questions concerning the interpersonal communication behavior patterns of the person with whom you just interacted. Use the following scale:

        1 = definitely
        2 = probably
        3 = can't tell
        4 = probably not
        5 = definitely not

1. This person is apprenhensive when communicating in most situations: _____

*Cues used:* _____

2. This person is normally dominant in interpersonal interactions: _____

*Cues used:* _____

3. This person is normally assertive in most interpersonal interactions: _____

*Cues used:* _____

4. This person is now relaxed and comfortable: _____

*Cues used:* _____

5. This person is feeling good about himself/herself: _____

*Cues used:* _____

6. This person readily self-discloses to others: _____

*Cues used:* _____

**Relationship Predictions:**

1. This person would (definitely, probably, perhaps, probably not, definitely not) like to get to know me better and perhaps have coffee or a soda with me at some later

   time: _____

*Cues used:* _____

2. This person (definitely did, probably did, perhaps did, probably did not, definitely

   did not) enjoy this encounter: _____

*Cues used:* _____

## First Impressions Self-Report Form

Respond to the following questions about yourself:

**Identifying data:**

1. Name _____

2. Age _____

3. Occupation and/or college major _____

4. Relational status _____

5. Political orientation _____

6. Music preferences _____

**Some Attitudes:**

Using the same scale as previously (1 = strongly agree; 2 = agree; 3 = relatively neutral; 4 = disagree; 5 = strongly disagree), respond to each of the following in terms of the extent to which you agree or disagree with each of the following:

1. The legalization of marijuana _____

2. Gay and lesbian rights bills_____

3. Mandatory retirement at age 65 _____

4. Setting the legal drinking age at 21 _____

5. Equal Rights Amendment (ERA) _____

**Interpersonal Communication Patterns**

Using the same scale as previously (1 = definitely; 2 = probably; 3= don't know or am not sure; 4 = probably not; 5 = definitely not), respond to each of the following concerning your interpersonal communication behavior patterns:

1. I am normally apprehensive when communicating: _____

2. I am normally dominant in interpersonal situations: _____

3. I am normally assertive in interpersonal interactions: _____

4. I am now relaxed and comfortable: _____

5. I am feeling good about myself: _____

6. I readily self-disclose to others: _____

**Relationship Predictions:**

1. I would (definitely, probably, perhaps, probably not, definitely not) like to get to know this person better and perhaps have a drink with him/her at some later time.

_____

2. I (definitely did, neither did nor didn't, didn't, definitely didn't) enjoy this

   interaction. _____

After both forms have been completed, exchange forms with the other person so that each may see what impressions were formed and how accurate/inaccurate they were. Discuss with your interactant, the specific cues used in forming impressions. The more specific you can be in identifying these cues, the more valuable this exercise will prove.

After you have discussed the impressions and the cues, the following principles may be considered:

► We cannot not communicate. Regardless of what we do or do not do, when in an interactional situation, we communicate to another person. Even silence communicates.

► All communication is self-reflexive. Regardless of what we talk about (or do not talk about), we communicate something about ourselves. We are forever telling others who we are, what we like and do not like, and a great deal more.

► We utilize a wide variety of cues in forming impressions of other people. Clothing, hair, gestures, jewelry, tone of voice, eye movements, facial expressions, and many other cues are used to draw inferences about who the person is and what the person is like. At the same time, others are using these same cues to draw inferences about us.

► First impressions are formed very quickly. In this exercise, we formed impressions of others in five minutes. Often, our impressions are formed even more quickly. We draw inferences about a person from merely seeing that person smile, frown, chew gum, or smoke a cigar. Others are just as quick to form impressions about us.

► First impressions are often long lasting and are often strongly resistant to change. First impressions often serve as filters through which everything else about that person is perceived. That is, our first impressions may influence the way in which we interpret that individual's future behavior. First impressions are thus extremely important in a wide variety of situations—in an interview, in meeting your blind date, in being introduced to your prospective in-laws, in meeting fellow students for the first time, and on and on.

*The general idea for this experience owes its formulation to an exercise that appeared in Jon A. Blaubaugh and Jim Quiggins, *Instructor's Manual to Accompany Patton and Giffin's Interpersonal Communication in Action*, 3d ed. (New York: Harper & Row, 1981) pp. 28-31.

## 1.2   An Introductory Quiz in Nonverbal Communication*

The purpose of this quiz is to introduce some of the areas of nonverbal communication that will be studied in this workbook and in this course and to stimulate your interest in nonverbal communication. Respond to each question with as many alternatives as you feel are correct. Each question may have one to four correct responses.

1. In the expression of feelings, the greatest impact of the message is due to:
   a. the verbal component
   b. the vocal component
   c. the facial component
   d. all of the above contribute equally to the message's total impact

2. If the communication signals you receive are contradictory, which would you most likely believe?
   a. facial cues
   b. vocal cues
   c. verbal cues
   d. all equally

3. A generally reliable nonverbal cue to A's being attracted to B is
   a. A gets physically close to B
   b. A mirrors or imitates B's behavior
   c. A smiles at B
   d. A maintains prolonged eye contact

4. The most important single factor influencing how much a person will like his or her date is
   a. the date's intelligence
   b. the date's sense of humor
   c. the date's physical attractiveness
   d. the date's personality attractiveness

5. Of the following, the one that is true is
   a. for both men and women, attractiveness had no bearing on happiness, self-esteem, and psychological health
   b. for men, attractiveness is positively related to happiness, self-esteem, and psychological health

    c. for women, atractiveness is positively related to happiness, self-esteem, and psychological health

    d. for men and women, attractiveness is negatively related to happiness, self-esteem, and psychological health

6. People demonstrate courtship cues (for example, preening, standing tall, high muscle tone, flirtatious glances) in
   a. romantic situations
   b. business meetings
   c. the college classroom
   d. the therapeutic encounter

7. College men like and are more attracted to women who are
   a. dressed up (skirt, blouse, and stockings) and wearing perfume
   b. dressed up and not wearing perfume
   c. dressed down (jeans) and wearing perfume
   d. dressed down and not wearing perfume

8. We can make fairly accurate predictions about personality on the basis of clothing behavior and clothing preferences for
   a. men
   b. women
   c. both men and women
   d. neither men nor women

9. Which of the following propositions regarding touch is true?
   a. mothers touch their children more than do fathers
   b. daughters touch their parents more than do sons
   c. men have a stronger desire to hold
   d. women have a stronger desire to be held

10. Of the following propositions relating to our tendency to avoid touch, the one(s) that is (are) true:
    a. older people show a greater tendency to avoid opposite sex touching
    b. men have a greater tendency to avoid same-sex touching than do women
    c. women have a greater tendency to avoid opposite sex touching than do men
    d. people who are low self-disclosives have a greater tendency to avoid touch

11. Of the following propositions concerning time communication, the one(s) that is (are) true:
    a. the more future oriented a person is the greater that person's income is likely to be
    b. parents from unskilled and semiskilled occupations usually socialize their children in a way that promotes an orientation to the present and a fatalistic and hedonistic perspective
    c. parents from the professional classes usually socialize their children in a way that promotes a future orientation along with strategies that are designed to promote success
    d. the orientation a person has toward time bears no relationship to future earnings or success

12. Of the following propositions concerning space communication, the one(s) that is (are) true:
    a. feminine markers (items that we leave somewhere to indicate that a seat or space belongs to us and that others should not use this seat or space) are more effective in repelling invaders than are masculine markers
    b. generally people will approach more closely and will maintain shorter distances with taller men than with shorter men
    c. one is less likely to invade the territory of two people than of four people; that is, the smaller the crowd, the less likely one is to invade it
    d. darkened rooms stimulate greater talking than do well-lighted rooms

13. Generally, large distances between people indicate:
    a. less acquaintance
    b. less friendliness
    c. less talkativeness
    d. less attractiveness

14. Of the following propositions concerning facial expressions the one(s) that is (are) true:
    a. all emotions are equally easy or difficult to display facially
    b. one cannot communicate two contradictory emotions such as sadness and happiness simultaneously
    c. women are better at displaying facial emotion than are men
    d. men are better at detecting facial emotions than are women

15. Eye movements can serve to
    a. monitor feedback
    b. signal a conversational turn
    c. signal the nature of a relationship

  d. compensate for physical distance

16. Generally, we find that people who talk fast (say, about twice as fast as normal), when compared to normal rate talkers, are generally
    a. more believable
    b. more efficient communicators
    c. less believable
    d. less efficient communicators

17. The best source of information about deception are
    a. foot and leg cues
    b. hand cues
    c. face cues
    d. verbal message cues

18. During relational deterioration, we would expect a decrease in
    a. rate of leg, foot, and self-touch movements
    b. frequency and duration of simultaneous speech
    c. rate of object manipulation during interaction
    d. rate of head, hand, and arm movements

19. Nonverbal involvement is greatest when a person is with a
    a. loved one
    b. friend
    c. stranger
    d. disliked other

20. Among the nonverbal gender differences are
    a. women evidence greater facial expressiveness
    b. women smile more when making negative statements
    c. women are smiled at more than men
    d. women maintain closer physical distances in interpersonal interactions

*The idea of a quiz to introduce the concepts or nonverbal communication was suggested by Don Stacks, Judee Burgoon, and Thomas Saine, Instructor's Manual for *The Unspoken Dialogue: An Introduction to Nonverbal Communication* (Boston, Mass.: Houghton Mifflin, 1978, p. 4).

# 1.3   The Areas of Nonverbal Communication

The purpose of this exercise is to introduce the major areas of nonverbal communication and to provide you with the opportunity to generate questions about these different areas as a way of illustrating the range and depth of nonverbal communication.

The areas of nonverbal communication are noted here with brief definitions. Although there are various ways of classifying nonverbal behaviors, the areas are listed here as they appear in the chapters of this workbook.

For each area of nonverbal communication, generate at least three questions to which you would like the answer. Sample questions are provided for each area.

## Body Communication

That area of nonverbal communication concerned with the messages communicated by one's body and by body movements and gestures.

**Sample Question:** Do people form different impressions on the basis of the speed with which people walk?

1.



2.



3.

## Facial and Eye Communication

That area of nonverbal communication by which messages are communicated by facial and eye movements.

20

**Sample Question:** Who smiles more, men or women?

1.


2.


3.


## Artifactual Communication

That area of nonverbal communication concerned with the messages that artifacts communicate. "Artifact" is used in an extremely broad sense here to include one's clothing, hair style, jewelry, perfume or cologne, furniture, art objects, etc.

**Sample Question:** What messages does long hair on a male communicate?

1.


2.


3.


## Spatial Communication (Proxemics and Territoriality)

Proxemics is that area of nonverbal communication concerned with the messages that our treatment of space communicates, for example, the distance we stand from another person, the ways in which we arrange our homes and offices, and the patterns we use to arrange our communities. Spatial communication is generally broadened to include territoriality (the ownership-like reaction we have to different territories, places, and objects), how one can encroach on the territories of others and how such encroachments may be responded to; and how we mark territories.

**Sample Question:** How is status communicated by one's office?

1.


2.


3.


## Tactile Communication (Haptics)

That area of nonverbal communication concerned with the messages that are communicated through the skin, through touching and being touched.

**Sample Question:** Do men or women touch more?

1.


2.


3.


## Paralanguage and Silence

Paralanguage is that area concerned with the vocal but nonverbal dimension of speech, for example, the rate, volume, pitch, resonance, pauses, and quality of one's voice and what these communicate. Silence is the absence of speech but not of communication; silence communicates just as surely as words.

**Sample Question:** Do we believe the person who talks at a normal rate more or less than the person who talks at a particularly rapid rate?

1.


2.


3.


## Smell Communication (Olfactics)

That area of nonverbal communication concerned with the sending and receiving of smells.

**Sample Question:** Do women (men) prefer their dates to wear cologne or perfume?

1.


2.


3.


## Temporal Communication (Chronemics)

That area of nonverbal communication concerned with the messages communicated through time: the ways in which we use time, our time preferences and their implications, the ways in which our biological clocks function, and the ways our culture deals with time.

**Sample Question:** Is it better to be oriented to the future or to the present?

1.


2.


3.

# 1.4  Verbal and Nonverbal Message Systems

We communicate with at least two major message systems, the verbal and the nonverbal. The purpose of this exercise is to explore the similarities and differences between these two messages systems. Presented below are some of the characteristics of the verbal message system.* Are these characteristics also present in the nonverbal message system, as you understand it at this point? Indicate in the spaces provided how the nonverbal message system is similar to or is different from the verbal message system on each of the following characteristics.

1. *Duality of patterning:* there are two levels of language: the individual sounds (called ''phonemes'') and the meaningful units the sounds form when they are combined; language consists of a small group of individual sounds that are combined to form larger units, called morphemes and words.

2. *Rule-governed:* the rules of grammar dictate the permissible and the nonpermissible sequences of words for forming sentences.

3. *Cultural-transmission:* the language we speak is learned from the culture in which one is raised; it is not innate (though the propensity to learn human language may have a biological base).

4. *Learnability:* every human language is equally learnable by any normal human being.

5. *Openness or productivity:* new words and especially new sentences (sentences that have never been uttered before) are created and understood without any difficulty by native speakers of the language.

6. *Displacement:* language can be used to talk about the past and future, as well as the present, and about remote events and places.

7. *Rapid-Fading:* speech signals fade rapidly; they are evanescent.

8. *Arbitrariness:* language signals are arbitrary; they do not possess any of the physical properties or characteristics of the things for which they stand.

9. *Vocal-Auditory Channel:* human language makes use of the vocal-auditory channel; language signals are emitted vocally and received by the auditory system.

10. *Semanticity:* some language signals refer to things in the real world; they have referents that we can perceive through our various senses.

11. *Total Feedback:* speakers receive their own messages through feedback, both auditory and kinesthetic.

12. *Reflexiveness:* human language may be used to talk about objects, people, and events in the real world as well as about language itself; it is potentially "metalinguistic."

13. *Interchangeability:* any human being can serve as both sender and receiver of human language signals.

14. *Discreteness:* human language consists of discrete rather than continuous signals; each human language signal differs from every other human language signal in kind or type; each language signal is separate and distinct from every other signal. Language signals are like an on-off light switch; either the light is on or it is off. There are no variations in degrees.

15. *Prevarication:* because human language is a displaced and open or productive system, speakers have the capacity to lie.

*These characteristics were originally proposed by the linguist, Charles F. Hockett, "The Problem of Universals in Language," in J.H. Greenberg, ed., *Universals of Language* (Cambridge, Mass.: M.I.T. Press, 1963).

# 1.5　The Functions of Nonverbal Communication

## Example Identification

Nonverbal researchers identify six major functions frequently served by nonverbal communication. In the space provided record one specific example that you have observed for each of these six functions.

*To accent:* to highlight or emphasize some part of the verbal message

*To complement:* to reinforce the verbal message

*To contradict:* to communicate a meaning opposite to that of the verbal message

*To regulate:* to control or to indicate one's desire to control the flow of verbal messages

*To repeat:* to restate the meaning of the verbal message

*To substitute:* to take the place of verbal messages

27

## Interaction Analysis

These six functions may be further explored by having the entire class observe a half-hour situation comedy or other similar interaction and as a group identify as many examples of these six nonverbal communication functions as possible.

## Discussion of Nonverbal Functions

1. Which functions do nonverbal messages serve most frequently?

2. Nonverbal researchers have observed that we are easily held accountable for our verbal messages. That is, we would find it difficult to deny having said something. With nonverbal messages, however, there is less accountability; it is relatively easy to deny having communicated a particular nonverbal message. And we can easily claim that the observer misunderstood our intentions or did not perceive our gestures or expressions accurately. Explain how accountability is related to these six functions of nonverbal communication.

3. Are there other functions (in addition to the six identified here) that nonverbal messages serve? Explain.

4. How do verbal messages serve these same six functions? Give examples of verbal statements that serve each of these functions. For example, in the statement ''As we entered the cave we spotted this truly huge menacing-looking bear'' *truly* and *huge* emphasize *bear* and thus serve the function of accenting.

# 1.6    Rule-Keeping and Rule-Breaking*

The general objective of this exercise is to become better acquainted with some of the "rules" of nonverbal communication and to analyze some of the effects of breaking such rules.

Just as we learn verbal language without explicit teaching we also learn nonverbal language — the rules for interacting nonverbally. Such rules could include the following:

1. Upon entering an elevator, turn to the door and stare at it or at the numbers indicating where the elevator is until your floor is reached.

2. When sitting in a cafeteria, take a seat as far away from the next person as possible.

3. When sitting next to other people (or in the general area), do not invade their private space with your body or your belongings.

4. When sitting directly across from people, do not stare at them (that is, directly at their eyes) for more than a second or two.

5. Members of the opposite sex should not stare at the various sexual parts of the other person's body while that person is watching you.

6. When strangers are talking, do not enter their group.

7. When talking with someone, do not stand too close or too far away. You may move closer when talking about intimate topics. Never stand close enough so that you can smell the other person's body odor. This rule may be broken only under certain conditions — for example, when the individuals involved are physically attracted to each other or when one individual is consoling another or when engaged in some game where the rules require this close contact.

8. When talking in an otherwise occupied area, lower your voice so that other people are not disturbed by your conversation.

9. When talking with others, look at their eyes and facial area only occasionally. Neither stare at them nor avoid their glance completely.

10. When talking with people, do not touch them more than absolutely necessary. This is especially important when the parties do not know each other. Some touching is permitted when the parties are well acquainted. Touching is more permissible for women than it is for men — that is, it is more permissible for women to touch women than for men to touch men.

## Procedure

The procedures are relatively simple. Groups of two students are formed; one student is designated as rule breaker and one is designated as observer.

The task of the rule breaker is simply to enter some situation where one or more rules of nonverbal communication would normally be operative and break one or more rules. The task of the observer is to record mentally (or in writing if possible) what happens as a result.

Each group should then return after a specified amount of time and report back to the entire class what happened.

Again, remember to observe the rights of others; do not engage in any experience that will embarrass or endanger another person.

*The idea for this exercise was first suggested to me by Jean Civikly, University of New Mexico.

# 1.7   Giving Instructions Nonverbally

The purpose of this exercise is to heighten your awareness of nonverbal communication.

The class is broken up into groups of five or six. One member from each group leaves the room for approximately one minute. While these "subjects" are out of the room, each group is given an instruction that they must communicate to the subject using only the nonverbal cue or cues to which they are restricted. All groups should of course be given the same instruction and be limited to the same verbal cue or cues so that the task will be equally difficult for all groups.

The first group to get the subject to comply with their instruction wins the round and gets 10 points. Then the process is repeated, this time with another subject chosen from the group, another instruction, and another nonverbal cue (or cues). The exercise is completed when one group wins 50 points, when time is up, or when some other predetermined point is reached.

Some sample instructions and types of nonverbal cues follow. Instructors may wish to compile their own list of instructions to ensure that they have not been seen by any member of the class.

## Sample Instructions

Leave the room; give the teacher a pat on the back; shake hands with each member of the group; open (close) all the windows; open (close) the door; bring into the class someone who is not a member of the class; write the time on the board; find a red pen; raise your hand; clap hands; sit on the floor; put your shoes on the wrong feet; get a drink of water; hold up a notebook with a name of the school on it; comb your hair.

## Nonverbal Cues

Vocal (but nonverbal) cues; hand and arm movements; eye movements (but not head movements); head movements; movements of the entire body; manipulation of the entire body; tactile cues; manipulation of objects in the room; leg movements (including feet movements).

# 1.8  Approaches to Nonverbal Communication

Although a number of approaches to nonverbal communication may be identified, two approaches or orientations are especially significant: the structural and the clinical. Some of the major differences are:

**Structural Approach**

1. Nonverbal communication is an area inseparable from communication in general.

2. The general goal of nonverbal communication study is to understand the process of communication.

3. Researchers are most concerned with the identification of the units of nonverbal communication and with how they fit together, that is, their pattern or grammar.

4. Nonverbal behaviors are related to each other and depend, for their meaning, on the context and the other nonverbal behaviors with which they occur.

**Clinical Approach**

1. Nonverbal behavior is a separate area of study.

2. The general goal of nonverbal communication study is to understand personality, to figure out what is going on inside the individual's head.

3. Researchers are not concerned with the identification of the units of nonverbal communication or with their ''grammar.''

4. Nonverbal behaviors have individual meanings; hence, individual units of nonverbal behavior may be studied and their meanings identified in isolation from the context and the other nonverbal behaviors with which they occur.

What approach does this workbook take? If you are using a standard textbook, what approach does the text take? Examine some specific chapters to determine the approach(es) the authors take. What evidence—in the form of specific passages from this workbook and/or from the textbook as well as specific statements identifying the approach taken—can you find to support your conclusions?

# Review and Discussion Questions

[*A Note on the Use of the Review and Discussion Questions:* These questions are designed to enable you to achieve two important goals: (1) to review the relevant theoretical material on nonverbal communication and (2) to consider extensions and applications of this material to your own lives. In each of the chapters roughly the first half of the questions addresses the review function and the second half addresses the application function. Consider each type of question. Each is important. Each provides a different perspective on this new and exciting area of nonverbal communication.]

1. What is nonverbal communication? Which definition presented in this unit, seems the most logical or the most reasonable? Why?

2. What are the major divisions or types of nonverbal communication? Are there other aspects of nonverbal communication not included here?

3. Describe the role of intentionality and nonintentionality in defining communication and especially nonverbal communication.

4. What are the major functions that nonverbal communication serves? Can you identify any function that nonverbal communication serves that is not included in the six functions identified in this chapter?

5. In what ways does nonverbal communication differ from verbal communication? For example, does nonverbal communication follow rules similar to the rules of grammar for verbal communication? Are nonverbal behaviors capable of communicating all types of information or are nonverbal behaviors unable to communicate certain types of information? Explain. Is nonverbal communication learned in essentially the same ways as verbal communication?

6. Which forms of nonverbal communication do you make use of most often? Explain?

7. How can a knowledge of nonverbal communication help you achieve your professional goal? How might its ineffective use hinder your achievement of this goal or other goals?

8. How can a knowledge of nonverbal communication help you interpersonally and in your close relationships?

9. What forms of nonverbal communication do you exhibit most effectively? What forms of nonverbal communication are in need of improvement? What might you do to effect these improvements?

# Terms to Define

[*A note on the Terms to Define:* These terms are included here to assist you in reviewing the most significant concepts in nonverbal communication. Generally, this section will prove most helpful if you (1) define these terms as specifically as possible, (2) consult a few different sources for the definitions (since different writers will define the terms somewhat differently and thereby provide slightly different perspectives on the same terms), and (3) record original examples along with the definitions. At the end of each list of terms to define is space to record any additional terms that you may encounter, either from readings or from class lectures and discussions. Record here any such terms along with relevant definitions and examples.]

Communication


Nonverbal communication


Body communication


Kinesics


Facial and eye communication


Artifactual communication


Proxemics


Territoriality

Tactile communication

Haptics

Paralanguage/paralinguistic

Silence

Olfaction/olfactics

Chronemics

Intentionality v. nonintentionality

Metacommunication/metalanguage

Additional relevant terms in nonverbal communication

# 2

# Body Communication

## Chapter Outline

Body Type
> Endomorphy, Mesomorphy, and
> Ectomorphy
> Body Type and Personality
> Impressions

Appearance and the Perception of
Attractiveness
> The Matching Hypothesis
> Compensation Theory
> Height

Body Movement and Gestures
> Emblems
> Illustrators
> Affect Displays
> Regulators
> Adaptors

Dimensions of Posture
> Inclusiveness/Noninclusiveness
> Face-to-Face/Parallel
> Congruence/Incongruence

Body Communication Exercises

2.1 Body Type Questionnaire
2.2 Body Type and Personality
    Impressions
2.3 Five Nonverbal Gestures
2.4 Some Meanings of Some Gestures
2.5 Body Awareness
2.6 Rules of Body Communication
2.7 Observational Record of Body
    Communication

Review and Discussion Questions
Terms to Define

## Objectives

After completing this chapter, you should be able to:

1. define the three major body types identified by Sheldon
2. explain the general stereotypes for each of the three body types
3. explain the matching hypothesis
4. explain compensation theory
5. define and give examples of each of the five types of gestures: *emblems, illustrators, affect displays, regulators,* and *adaptors*
6. explain the three dimensions of body posture identified by Scheflen

Body communication takes place in at least two different ways. First, we communicate through our body type. Although we may not be willing to argue that people with certain body types have specific personalities *because* of their body types, we do know that others formulate different expectations on the basis of the different body types. Therefore, although a tall and muscular male may not be aggressive, many people will have this expectation based solely on his body type. Second, we communicate through our gross body movements and our gestures.

# Body Type

Body types are usually distinguished along three dimensions. Each person has all three dimensions but in different degrees and it is these differences in degrees that make for the different body types. The three dimensions are endomorphy, mesomorphy, and ectomorphy.

## Endomorphy, Mesomorphy, and Ectomorphy

Endomorphy is the fatty dimension. The short and stout individual would be the typical endomorph. Mesomorphy is the muscular dimension and would be characteristic of the body of the body builder or athlete. Ectomorphy is the thinness dimension; the tall, thin individual would be the typical ectomorph. As already noted, we all have these three dimensions. Some of us, however, are particularly high on endomorphy whereas others are particularly high on mesomorphy. Usually, body types are identified with the three digit number (with each number ranging from a low of 1 to a high of 7) signifying the degree to which each of these dimensions is present in a particular body. Taking the dimensions in the order given (endomorphy, mesomorphy, and ectomorphy) we might say that the fat man in the circus would be a 7-1-1, indicating that this person is extremely high on the endomorphic dimensions but extremely low on the muscular and the skinny dimensions. Arnold Schwartzenegger or Mr. Olympia would be described as 1-7-1, indicating extremely high muscularity but little fattiness and little skinniness. Last, the thin man in the circus would be described as 1-1-7—little fattiness, little muscularity, much thinness. Of course, these are extremes but you can easily develop three-digit descriptors for any individual or type of individual.

## Body Type and Personality Impressions

The original research on body type, conducted on males rather than both sexes, attempted to correlate body type and personality. Certain body types were assumed to have certain personality types. Viscerotonia is characterized by slow reactions, a love of comfort, sociability, food, and affection, and an easy going temperament. Viscerotonia was especially associated with endomorphic body types. Somatotonia—associated with the mesomorphic body type—is characterized by risk-taking and physicality. This person is aggressive, courageous, adventurous, and dominant. Cerebrotonia, characteristic of ectomorphic body types, is associated with a secretiveness and a self-consciousness. This person avoids attracting attention to oneself and generally prefers solitude. Much as the three body types could be described with a three digit number, so could these personality types. The numbers, according to William Sheldon who pioneered in this research, should be similar. Thus, a person with a 2-6-5 body type should have a 2-6-5 personality type as well.

Much of this research has been discredited but one thing is clear: we formulate personality impressions on the basis of a person's body type. We expect people with certain body types to have certain personality characteristics. If you are not convinced of this try the exercise "Body Type and Personality Impression."

# Appearance and the Perception of Attractiveness

There can be little doubt that one's physical appearance contributes significantly to the perception of attractiveness. Likewise, there can be little doubt that people judged attractive are perceived much more favorably in a wide variety of situations. Here are just a few examples.

For example, therapists-in-training responded to attractive clients with greater warmth and supportiveness than to their less attractive clients. In a study using photographs of persons varying in attractiveness, it was found that the more attractive persons were judged as sexually warmer, more responsive, kinder, more poised, more modest, stronger, more sensitive, more sociable, more outgoing, more happily married, employed in more prestigious jobs, and more likely to be competent husbands and wives.

Elementary school teachers who were shown *identical* report cards accompanied by pictures varying in terms of attractiveness judged the more attractive students' reports as indicating higher educational potential, having better social relationships with peers, having parents who were more interested in their children's education, and having higher I.Q.s.

Responses from attractive people seem to mean more than responses from unattractive people. For example, in one study a female clinician was made up to look beautiful for interacting with certain groups and unattractive for interacting with other groups. The "beautiful" clinician's diagnoses, it was found, meant a great deal more to the individuals to whom they were given than did the diagnoses given by the "unattractive" clinician.

Not surprisingly, attractive persons indicate a greater degree of satisfaction and pleasure from their interpersonal interactions than do less attractive persons.

It is clear that the attractive person has the edge. Clearly, we respond more favorably to attractive than to unattractive people. However, we also find that as our degree of liking for a person increases, so does our perception of their attractiveness. Liking and attractiveness seem to influence each other.

## The Matching Hypothesis

Much research has supported what has come to be called the "matching hypothesis." This hypothesis states that we date and mate those people who are approximately equal to ourselves in attractiveness. That is, we select persons for dating and mating who are neither much more attractive nor much less attractive than ourselves. You may wish see if this is true in the relationships with which you are familiar and to speculate on the reasons for this matching tendency.

## Compensation Theory

There are, of course, times when an unattractive person and an attractive person do date and mate. Generally, when we see this we secretely wonder what accounts for this unmatched pairing. What compensation is the less attractive person offering? Money probably comes to mind most quickly. Power and status probably come next in importance. Personality, a sense of humor, warmth, supportiveness and all the other qualities we consider significant in a relational partner are also important, although they do not seem as important as money, power, and status.

## Height

A special aspect of appearance—height—deserves to be emphasized. Generally, the research literature indicates a decided preference for taller rather than shorter people. Here are a few examples. When corporate recruiters were shown identical resumes for people some of whom were noted as being 5'5'' and others as being 6'1'', the taller individual was chosen significantly more often than were the shorter individuals.

In another study, the salaries of college graduates from the University of Pittsburgh were analyzed. It was found that the salaries of those between 6'2'' to 6'4'' were 12.4 percent higher than the salaries of those under 6'.

In all presidential elections since 1900, with the one exception of Ford (6'1'') and Carter (5'9 1/2''), the taller candidate won. Do we favor the taller individual to the extent that we vote this person into the highest office in the country?

In an investigation of height and satisfaction it was found, and not surprisingly, that boys were less satisfied with their heights than were girls. Fifty percent of the boys surveyed indicated that they wanted to be taller; 2 percent said they wanted to be shorter; and 48 percent indicated satisfaction. Only 20 of the girls indicated that they wanted to be taller; 13 percent said they wanted to be shorter; and 67 percent indicated that they were satisfied.

Preferences for different heights seem culturally determined and greatly influenced by the media and fashion trends. Today, tall is in. For both men and women tallness seems to be a decided asset. On television and in fashion ads, tall people seem favored, despite such obvious exceptions as Michael J. Fox and Madonna.

# Body Movement and Gestures

"Body communication" takes place through both our gross body movements (the way we walk, stand, or sit) and our smaller movements or gestures (the way we shake hands, wave, or point).

One of the most widely used systems of body movements divides these movements into five classes: emblems, illustrators, affect displays, regulators, and illustrators.

---

We respond to gestures with an extreme alertness and, one might almost say, in accordance with an elaborate and secret code that is written nowhere, known to none, and understood by all.

Edward Sapir

---

## Emblems

*Emblems* are nonverbal behaviors that rather directly translate words or phrases, for example, the O.K. sign or the "V" for victory sign. They are performed with conscious awareness and are, unlike many other gestures, always intentional. Further, emblems are culture-specific; they are not universal. When then President Nixon visited Latin America and gestured with the "O.K." sign he thought signified something positive, he was quickly informed that this gesture was not universal. In Latin America it is equivalent to our "screw you."

## Illustrators

*Illustrators* accompany and literally "illustrate" the verbal messages, for example, the pointing gesture. Most illustrators are hand gestures but we also illustrate with our head, shoulders, and with our entire body. We illustrate our talk in a variety of ways: pointing to what we are talking about ("that's the building I want to live in"), drawing pictures in the air ("it was shaped like an egg"), and indicating size or spatial relationships ("the baby was real small").

## Affect Displays

*Affect displays* are the movements of the facial area that convey emotional meaning. Affect displays may be used with verbalizations but may also be used independently. Some researchers have speculated that since the right brain is concerned with feelings and since the left side of the body is controlled by the right brain that left hand and body gestures will be concerned with feelings. The right hand and body gestures, on the other hand, will more likely communicate logical relationships and meanings since they are controlled by the left brain which controls the logical part of us. Some theorists have extended this argument to say that since women are more right brain oriented, they will gesture more with the left hand and the left side of their body. Men, on the other hand, since they are left-brain dominated will gesture more with the right hand and the right side of their body. How would you go about testing these theories?

## Regulators

*Regulators* monitor, maintain, control, or coordinate the speaking of another individual, for example, the head nod that tells the speaker to keep on speaking.

## Adaptors

*Adaptors* are nonverbal gestures by which we touch ourselves, the person to whom we are speaking, or some object, for example, our tie or necklace. Generally, self-touching behaviors are emitted more in stressful situations and are generally thought to indicate some kind of discomfort or negative feeling.

*As the tongue speaketh to the ear, so the hand speaketh to the eye.*

*Francis Bacon*

# Dimensions of Posture

Nonverbal researcher Albert Scheflen has identified three dimensions of posture along which any given postural position may be analyzed: inclusiveness/noninclusiveness, face-to-face/parallel; and congruence/incongruence.

These labels identify the extremes; do realize that between these extremes there are a large number of body posture positions possible. What we are describing, then, are postural tendencies toward one end or the other of these three dimensions. These three dimensions are generally sufficient for analyzing and describing postural positioning in interpersonal interactions.

Note that this is not the same as saying that we can therefore identify what is going on in the minds of the individuals or that we can therefore know how they feel about each other. In reading the following descriptions, visualize two people sitting on a couch together.

## Inclusiveness/Noninclusiveness

This dimension refers to the degree to which one person's body posture includes the other person exclusively. At the high inclusiveness end of the scale, we would have one person's body posture being arranged so as to include the other person on the couch but to exclude all others from the interaction. At the noninclusiveness end, we would have body posture that does not include the other person on the couch and also does not exclude any other members.

High inclusiveness is generally found in situations where the individuals are involved in an intimate relationship or are engaged in some very private and personal conversation. Rarely would high inclusiveness be found with persons who dislike each other or who are unfriendly toward each other.

## Face-to-Face/Parallel

This dimension refers to the degree to which the two people face each other directly (face-to-face) or position themselves so that their shoulders are in the same line, for example, both sitting on the couch facing forward. Face-to-face positioning is used when the individuals are mutually involved as they would be in an intimate discussion. Parallel positioning might be seen if the two persons were watching television or reading.

When we are uncomfortable with or dislike another person, we tend to avoid face-to-face interaction. As our degree of comfort and liking increase, we seem to move closer and closer to face-to-face positioning.

## Congruence/Incongruence

This dimension refers to the degree to which one person mirrors or imitates the behavior of the other person. In high congruence, the two persons would mirror each other's behavior. In low congruence (or incongruence) the behaviors of one person are not imitated by the other. In fact, in incongruent situations, one person may engage in behavior that is opposite to the behaviors of the other person. For example, in an incongruent situation, if one person leans forward the other person may lean back.

Congruence, mirroring, or behavioral synchrony (the terms mean essentially the same thing) generally indicate a high degree of attraction and liking of one person for the other. Incongruence, on the other hand, generally indicates little attraction and little liking. But, do be careful in applying this general principle to analyze interpersonal interactions. There are a great number of other factors that have to be taken into consideration. Remember the principle of packaging; we cannot (and should not) draw inferences from any one bit of nonverbal behavior without taking into consideration the entire package of signals (verbal as well as nonverbal).

# Body Communication Exercises

The exercises contained in this chapter focus on increasing our understanding of the ways in which we send and receive meanings on the basis of body type and body movement. The first exercise, *Body Type Questionnaire*, enables you to test out some of the relationships between body type and personality by analyzing yourself. In *Body Type and Personality Impressions* we explore our own stereotypes concerning body types.

In *Five Nonverbal Gestures* and *Some Meanings of Some Gestures* we further explore how gestures communicate a wide variety of messages. In *Body Awareness* we explore the relationship between feelings and body movements. Can we, for example, change our feelings through our body movements? The rule-governed nature of body communication is the focus of *Rules of Body Communication*. The *Observational Record of Body Communication* encourages you to increase your own awareness of how you send and receive messages from body type and movement.

## 2.1 Body Type Questionnaire*

Instructions: Fill in each blank with a word from the suggested list following each statement. For any blank, three in each statement, you may select any word from the list of twelve immediately below. An exact word to describe you may not be in the list, but select the words that seem to fit most closely the way you are.

1. I feel most of the time _____ , _____ , and _____ .

   **calm, anxious, cheerful, contented, relaxed, confident, tense, impetuous, complacent, reticent, energetic, self-conscious**

2. When I study or work, I seem to be _____ , _____ , and _____ .

   **efficient, enthusiastic, reflective, placid, sluggish, competitive, leisurely, meticulous, precise, determined, thoughtful, cooperative**

3. Socially, I am _____ , _____ , and _____ .

   **outgoing, affable, tolerant, gentle-tempered, considerate, awkward, affected, soft-tempered, argumentative, shy, talkative, hot-tempered**

4. I am rather _____ , _____ , and _____ .

   **active, warm, domineering, introspective, forgiving, courageous, suspicious, cool, sympathetic, serious, soft-hearted, enterprising**

5. Other people consider me rather _____ , _____ , and _____ .

   **generous, adventurous, withdrawn, dominant, optimistic, affectionate, reckless, detached, sensitive, kind, cautious, dependent**

6. For letters A through F below, underline the one word of the three selections which most closely describes the way you are:

   A. **assertive, relaxed, tense**
   B. **hot-tempered, cool, warm**
   C. **withdrawn, sociable, active**
   D. **confident, tactful, kind**
   E. **dependent, dominant, detached**
   F. **enterprising, affable, anxious**

The next step in completing this questionnaire-analysis is to locate the words you selected and underlined from the three lists provided here. Total the number of words you selected from each of the three columns: endomorphy, mesomorphy, and ectomorphy. These relative totals should reflect your own body type. Do they? How much do they differ from your perception of yourself?

| Endomorphy | Mesomorphy | Ectomorphy |
|---|---|---|
| affable | active | anxious |
| affected | adventurous | awkward |
| affectionate | argumentative | cautious |
| calm | assertive | considerate |
| complacent | cheerful | cool |
| contented | competitive | detached |
| cooperative | confident | gentle-tempered |
| dependent | courageous | introspective |
| forgiving | determined | meticulous |
| generous | dominant | precise |
| kind | domineering | reflective |
| leisurely | efficient | reticent |
| placid | energetic | self-conscious |
| relaxed | enterprising | sensitive |
| sluggish | enthusiastic | serious |
| sociable | hot-tempered | shy |
| soft-hearted | impetuous | suspicious |
| soft-tempered | optimistic | tactful |
| sympathetic | outgoing | tense |
| tolerant | reckless | thoughtful |
| warm | talkative | withdrawn |

*This test of body type comes from J. B. Cortes and F. M. Gatti, "Physique and Self-Description of Temperament," *Journal of Consulting Psychology* 29 (1965): 408-414. For additional information on this test and its implications see this article.

## 2.2  Body Type and Personality Impression

When William Sheldon first published his findings on body type and personality, he proposed that we could effectively analyze certain aspects of personality on the basis of one's body type. Whether one can do so validly and reliably has been the subject of much research and theory since Sheldon's original publications. However, we do seem to *expect* certain body types to have specific personality characteristics, whether or not they do in fact possess these characteristics.

The three major body types are:

Endomorph:  short, fat

Ectomorph:   tall, thin

Mesomorph:  muscular, athletic

The objective of this exercise is to identify the type of body with which you would expect the following personality characteristics to be associated.

| Personality characteristic | Expected body type |
|---|---|
| 1. Warmhearted | 1. |
| 2. Tense | 2. |
| 3. Masculine | 3. |
| 4. Ambitious | 4. |
| 5. Old-fashioned | 5. |
| 6. Sympathetic | 6. |
| 7. Adventurous | 7. |
| 8. Trusting | 8. |
| 9. Nervous | 9. |
| 10. Mature | 10. |
| 11. Dependent | 11. |
| 12. Pessimistic | 12. |
| 13. Sympathetic | 13. |
| 14. Self-reliant | 14. |
| 15. Quiet | 15. |

**For Discussion:**

1. What degree of *intra*subject reliability would you expect on this type of task? That is, to what extent would you agree with yourself if you completed this task at another time, say, two or three months from now? Explain.

2. What degree of *inter*subject reliability would you expect on this type of task? That is, to what extent would you agree with others who completed this same task? Test out your prediction by comparing your responses with those of others. Are there certain personality characteristics for which intersubject reliability would be especially high and others for which it would be especially low? Explain.

3. What does this experience tell you about the expectations or impressions that people formulate about you? How might you go about changing or modifying such impressions?

## 2.3 Five Nonverbal Gestures

**Definitions and Examples:**

Define each of the following terms and identify at least one specific example of each of these nonverbal gestures.

*Emblem*

*Illustrator*

*Regulator*

*Affect Display*

*Adaptor*

**Interaction Analysis:**

Observe five or ten minutes of an interaction (a soap opera is especially appropriate here although any interpersonal interaction should do) and identify examples of each of these five gestures.

**Discussion of the Five Gestures:**

1. Which of these five gestures are intentional? Which are *usually* unintentional? Which can be either?

2. Which of these five gestures only occur with verbalization? Which may occur with or without verbalization?

3. Which of these five gestures are cross-cultural? Which are culture specific?

4. Do men and women differ in their use of any of these five gestures? Explain.

# 2.4  Some Meanings of Some Gestures

This exercise is designed to illustrate just a few of the wide range of emblems that are used throughout the world. Further, the difficulty of this exercise should make clear that the meanings of emblems cannot be deduced from a logical analysis of the form of the gesture. These particular emblems were taken from a study by Desmond Morris, Peter Collett, Peter Marsh, and Marie O'Shaughnessy (*Gestures: Their Origins and Distribution*, New York: Stein and Day, 1979) which concentrated on the Mediterranean area.

Match the meanings presented on page fifty-five with the illustrations on page fifty-four. After you have completed these matchings individually, it may prove interesting to interact in a small group of five or six others to compare and revise your matchings. Since these emblems are taken from a variety of different cultures, working in a group (especially one representing a variety of cultures) will probably provide the additional insights needed for many of the correct matchings.

Note that the meanings provided for these emblems are presented in the order of frequency with which respondents supplied them. Thus, for example, in "A," the most frequently given response for a particular emblem was "victory." "Two" was the next most frequent response, and so on.

_____ A. Victory, two, sexual insult, horns

_____ B. Sexual comment, sexual insult, protection, nose joke

_____ C. O.K./good, orifice, zero, threat

_____ D. Sexual insult, sexual comment, strength

_____ E. Thin & ill, attractive, thinking, success, sad, threat, crafty, effeminate

_____ F. Complicity, be alert, you are nosey, I am clever, he is clever, threat

_____ G. Query, good, fear, lots, emphasis, criticism, slowly

_____ H. Departure demand, departure description, departure request

_____ I. I am alert, be alert, praise, complicity, boredom

_____ J. Good, effeminate, crazy, crafty

_____ K. Cuckold, general insult, protection, curse

_____ L. Praise, salutation

_____ M. Mockery

_____ N. Effeminate, warning, good, sponger, protection, informer, disbelief

_____ O. Nothing, anger, praise

_____ P. Protection, O.K./good, break friendship, friendship, swear oath, compilation

_____ Q. Negative, beckon, antagonism, superiority, query, salutation, rejection, directional

_____ R. O.K., one, sexual insult, hitch-hike, directional

_____ S. Disinterest, negative, disbelief

_____ T. Cuckold, protection, insult, threat, curse

## 2.5  Body Awareness

The purpose of this exercise is to heighten your awareness of how your body acts and feels as a result of different emotions and to raise the question of whether your feelings can be altered by body movement and expressions. For two minutes, role play the following emotions:


Happiness


Sadness


Expectancy


Fear


Surprise


Identify at least three qualities of your nonverbal behavior that characterized each of these emotions. Did this role playing influence your feelings? What conclusions would you draw concerning the connection between emotions and body movements as a result of this experience?

## 2.6 Rules of Body Communication

Identify three rules of *body communication and gesture* operating in our culture that are uniquely "masculine." [Note: rules may be conceived of as prescriptive (indicating what should be done) or as proscriptive (indicating what should not be done).]

1.

2.

3.

Identify three rules of *body communication and gestures* operating in our culture that are uniquely "feminine."

1.

2.

3.

Identify three rules of *body communication and gesture* that will distinguish the high status from the low status individual in an interpersonal interaction.

1.

2.

3.

Review the nine rules you have identified and respond to the following:

1. What do these rules communicate about men, about women, and about the relationship between men and women in our culture?

2. Do you think these rules are changing? In what direction? Why are(n't) they changing?

3. Do you think these rules are cross-cultural or culture specific? If possible, provide examples of the same rules or contradictory rules operating in other cultures.

## 2.7   Observational Record of Body Communication

This observational record form is designed to increase your awareness of the forms and functions of body communication and its role in the total communication act. For each example of body communication noted, (1) describe the specific manifestation of that communication, and indicate (2) the sources and receivers of the message; (3) the specific context in which the communication occurred; (4) the message or meanings that were communicated; (5) the effects of the nonverbal communication; and (6) any additional comments or questions that you feel are relevant to understanding the specific communication.

Emblem:

Illustrator:

Adaptor:

Affect Display:

Regulator:

Endomorph:

Mesomorph:

Ectomorph:

# Review and Discussion Questions

1. What are the three major body types as identified by William Sheldon and their corresponding personality expectations? What evidence can you advance for or against Sheldon's assumptions from your own experiences?

2. How do advertisers use these three body types to convey their desired message? Can you cite a specific advertisement thathelps to reinforce this "connection" between body build and personal characteristics?

3. Do you have different expectations for the different body types? What are they? How do you suppose you developed these expectations?

4. What messages does your body type communicate to others? What messages do your body movements communicate to others?

5. What physical qualities do you look for in your "ideal mate"? Why do you single out these qualities? What role does attractiveness play in your dating behaviors? Why? How effective is the matching hypothesis in predicting who will date and mate whom? What evidence from your own experiences can you bring to bear on this hypothesis? When the matching hypothesis does not hold, do you normally look for compensating factors?

6. Do you find that people do favor tall people over shorter people? In what ways?

7. Are body movements and gestures innate or learned? Are some innate and some learned? What evidence would you need to draw valid and reliable conclusions concerning the innate versus the learned issue?

8. How satisfied are you with your body? Consider, at least: hair, eyes, facial features, skin (color, complexion, tone), height, weight, general body build, muscle tone, chest, arms, hands, legs, and waist. Do you communicate to others your relative degree of satisfaction-dissatisfaction? How? How might you go about improving the body parts with which you're not so satisfied?

9. Of what value is Scheflen's analysis of posture? Do you make use of these categories or dimensions when you make inferences about other people? Explain.

# Terms to Define

Body type

Endomorph

Mesomorph

Ectomorph

Matching hypothesis

Compensation theory

Emblems

Illustrators

Affect displays

Regulators

Adaptors

Inclusiveness/noninclusiveness

Face-to-face/parallel

Congruence/Incongruence

Mirroring

Behavioral synchrony

Additional relevant terms in body communication

# 3

# Facial and Eye Communication

## Objectives

After completing this chapter, you should be able to:

1. define and explain *affect displays*
2. explain the nature of micromomentary expressions
3. explain the universal and the relative positions on the facial communication of emotions
4. define and give examples of each of the four facial management techniques: intensifying, deintensifying, neutralizing, and masking
5. explain at least four of the styles in facial expression identified by Ekman and Friesen
6. identify at least three functions of eye contact
7. explain the nature of *civil inattention*
8. define *pupillometrics*

Here we focus on the face—the various movements we make with our faces, for example, the smiles and the frowns—and especially on the eyes.

The face is the most compelling channel of nonverbal communication and also one which poses some of the most challenging issues for the field. Most of us equate our social identity with our facial appearance. Photographs of the face alone suffice for full identification, and we ordinarily can recognize others by their facial features alone. Imputations of character and beauty often center exclusively on the face. Injuries to the face are seen as an unusually severe type of social disability . . . affecting the very sense of self and ability to survive in a social environment. We attend almost exclusively to the face in interaction and are aware that others are monitoring our facial appearance as well.

Weitz, p. 17

# Facial Expressions

The face is surely our most expressive instrument and the one from which we derive the most meaning. It is the first thing we look at when we meet someone new and probably the single most important physical attribute in our assessment of attractiveness.

## Affect Displays

Facial gestures are primarily responsible for communicating a wide variety of emotions and feelings. Among the emotions generally agreed to be facially communicated, in what are referred to as *primary affect displays*, are happiness, surprise, fear, anger, sadness, and disgust/ contempt. Other researchers would add to this list bewilderment and determination.

In addition, there are *affect blends*, facial displays that are combinations of these various primary emotions. For example, we may experience both happiness and sadness at the same time; the happiness may be signaled by the lower face while the sadness may be signaled by the upper face.

Some emotions are easier to display and to detect than others. For example, it has been found that happiness is easier to detect than is sadness. Further, women are better at both displaying and detecting facial emotions.

## Micromomentary Expressions

Some research suggests that we frequently manifest emotions facially in extremely short periods of time. In fact, the time during which these emotions are displayed is so short that the facial expressions resist detection without the aid of slow motion films. These emotions, some researchers would argue, are especially revealing of one's true feelings.

## Universality or Relativity

One of the more interesting questions concerning facial expressions is whether they are universal or relative. Do all people throughout the world communicate their emotions facially in the same way (the universal position) or are there great variations from one culture to another (the relative position)? Research conducted on children who were born blind has found that these children communicate their emotions facially in the same way that sighted children do, despite the fact that the blind children have never had the opportunity to learn these expressions from their adult community. This research, then, supports the univeralist position. Other research seems to indicate that different cultures express the emotions in different ways and that therefore facial expressions are relative and differ from one culture to another. It may be that the observed differences are actually a reflection of what is permissible and what is not permissible to communicate in the culture. For example, in some cultures it is permissible to show contempt openly. In other cultures this is not permissible.

# Facial Management Techniques

Because our face responds so readily to our inner feelings, reflecting perhaps what we want to keep hidden, we often engage in what are called "facial management techniques," techniques designed to communicate something a bit differently from what we are really feeling. Nonverbal researchers Paul Ekman and Wallace Friesen identify four major techniques: intensifying, deintensifying, neutralizing, and masking.

---

**Face—the mirror of the mind.**

St. Jerome, *Letter 54*

---

## Intensifying

We engage in intensifying facial management when we wish to exaggerate an expression of emotion that we are feeling. Let's say Grandma gives you a $50 Savings Bond. Though you expected more, you are pleased and want to let Grandma feel extra good and so exaggerate your joy at getting the Bond. Your eyes grow wider than they would normally and you smile more broadly than you would if it arrived in the mail where no one would see your response.

## Deintensifying

Deintensifying is the logical opposite of intensifying and occurs when we feel an emotion strongly but reduce the strength of its reflection in our face. Assume, for example, that you and a friend have each applied for a scholarship to graduate school. You both open your letters at the same time; you have received the scholarship, your friend has not. You would probably feel very happy for yourself, a happiness that would normally be reflected in your facial expression. But, because you don't want to make matters worse for your friend, you might deintensify your expression of happiness.

> **Frequently we place considerable reliance on facial cues when making important interpersonal judgements. This begins when, as infants, we take special interest in the huge face peering over our crib and tending to our needs.**
>
> **Knapp, p. 263**

## Neutralizing

In neutralization we try to hide any outward expression of felt emotions. In our culture, men are generally supposed to engage in greater neutralizing than women who, for example, are allowed freedom to cry, to express elation, and to register fear facially. In various card games, neutralizing (the "poker face") is an important skill carefully cultivated by serious players.

## Masking

In masking we replace or substitute the expression of one emotion for the expression of another emotion. For example, we might be afraid but instead of registering fear on our faces, we substitute a happy expression (and perhaps even whistle). We see masking when the shy and unsure teenager asks for a date. Too afraid to communicate this unsureness, the teenager feigns cockiness.

Actors, by definition and by occupation, practice facial management techniques throughout their careers. Others of us also practice, although in more informal and in more subtle ways.

# Styles in Facial Expression

In *Unmasking the Face*, nonverbal researchers Paul Ekman and Wallace Friesen identify eight styles of facial expression. According to Ekman and Friesen, these styles are essential and integral parts of an individual's personality. As a result, these styles will be present in a wide variety of situations (perhaps everywhere) over a long period of time (perhaps always). You may find it interesting to think of people you know—whether personal acquaintances, film or television personalities, or characters in literature—who represent these several styles.

*The Withholder.* This person displays little to no emotion. It has been argued that this lack of expression reinforces the behavior and becomes a contributing factor in inhibiting the experiencing of various emotions.

*The Revealer.* This person, the opposite of the withholder, displays all emotional feelings without any attempt to engage in any of the facial management techniques.

*The Unwitting Expressor.* This person displays feelings without realizing it. Often this person assumes that he or she was effective in hiding any expression of the felt emotions and frequently wonders how others knew how they were feeling.

*The Blanked Expressor.* Whereas the unwitting expressor expresses feelings without wishing to, the blanked expressor wishes to but doesn't. This person thinks he or she is expressing the felt emotions but only a relatively blank expression is actually displayed.

*The Substitute Expressor.* This person thinks he or she is communicating one emotion but is actually communicating a very different emotion. Whether this person is really feeling both emotions, only the emotion he or she is consciously aware of, or only the emotion that is actually expressed does not seem clear at this time.

*The Frozen-Affect Expressor.* This person always manifests the same emotion. Regardless of what is being felt, the same basic "frozen" expression is displayed.

*The Ever-Ready Expressor.* This person has the same particular expression ready for initial display at all times. Regardless of the

> [Oculesics is] the study of the communicative aspects of eye behavior.
>
> Richmond, McCroskey, and Payne, p. 11.

circumstances or the appropriateness of the expression, this person responds first and always with the same emotion. This is then followed by a more appropriate expression.

*The Flooded-Affect Expressor.* In all circumstances, this person displays one emotion (that is generally characteristic of the individual) mixed with another (usually more appropriate) emotion. For example, the person might display annoyance and, when feeling surprise, would display both annoyance and surprise.

## Eye Movements

Like the face, the eyes can communicate a great deal depending on the duration, direction, and quality of the eye movements. For example, when we exceed the normal time period for gazing at a stranger, we communicate something special. Generally, we find that when we like someone we maintain longer, more frequent, and more direct eye contact.

> Drink to me only with thine eyes, and I will pledge with mine.
>
> Ben Jonson

## Eye Functions

Eye contact can signal a variety of messages. Here are just a few such messages:

1. feedback seeking messages ("What did you think of what I said?");
2. conversational turn cues ("Now, you speak.");
3. relational messages ("I love you."); and
4. messages that compensate for long distances ("I want to be closer to you.").

## Eye Avoidance

We also use our eyes when we want to avoid interaction. For example, when we pass an arguing couple on the street, we often avert our eyes so as to say, "I didn't hear anything. Don't be embarrassed by me." Erving Goffman, in his Interaction Ritual, called this behavior "civil inattention."

Eye avoidance can also signal disinterest or an unwillingness to deal with an individual or a particular issue that the person wishes to discuss. Eye avoidance can also function to communicate disconfirmation of an individual, that is, it can communicate that this person does not matter to you, that you are indifferent to this person.

# Pupillometrics

Another area of eye behavior is known technically as *pupillometrics*, the study of the communicative function of pupil dilation and constriction. Generally, research finds that our pupils get larger or dilate when we are interested in or attracted to or feel positively toward what or whom we are watching. Thus, if we are looking at someone or something we find attractive, our pupils will get larger.

Generally, it has been found that we find people with large pupils more attractive than people with small pupils. This may be due to the fact that large pupils are simply more aesthetically pleasing. However, it may be due to the fact that since large pupils are a sign of attraction and liking that we perceive this person with large pupils to like us and hence like this person in return.

Conversely, our pupils get smaller or constrict when we are watching someone or something we are not attracted to or toward whom we feel negatively.

# Facial and Eye Communication Exercises

In *Facial Communication of Emotions* you are asked to work through the facial expression of a variety of emotions so that you will be in a better position to understand some of the research findings in this sometimes confusing area. Like all nonverbal communication, facial-expressions and eye movements may be said to follow certain rules; these are explored in *Rules of Facial and Eye Communication*.

In *The Effects of Eye Contact*, you are asked to communicate with different eye contact behaviors so as to appreciate first-hand the influence that eye movements have on communication. Much has been written about right brains and left brains and the differences between them. Some of these differences are explored in *Right and Left Movers*. As in other chapters, this one too contains a form to record your observations, *Observational Record of Facial and Eye Communication*.

# 3.1  Facial Communication of Emotions

Working in dyads or small groups, test the conclusion of Paul Ekman, Wallace Friesen, and Phoebe Ellsworth [*Emotion in the Human Face*: Guidelines for Research and an Integration of Findings that the face is capable of communicating the following eight "emotion categories": happiness, surprise, fear, anger, sadness, disgust, contempt, and interest.

On index cards, write the names of these emotion categories, one to a card. Place the cards face down on the desk and have one person select a card at random and attempt to communicate the emotion using only facial gestures. Keep a record of accurate and inaccurate guesses. Play until each emotion has been demonstrated at least twice. Then consider the following questions.

1. Do you agree with Ekman, Friesen, and Ellsworth that the face can communicate these eight emotion categories? What evidence would you use to support your answer?

2. Are some emotions easier to communicate than others? Why do you suppose this is true?

3. Dale Leathers, in *Nonverbal Communication Systems*, suggests that in addition to the eight emotions noted here, the face is also capable of communicating bewilderment and determination. Test out this suggestion in any way that seems useful and valid to you. Explain your conclusion and the evidence you would use to support your conclusion.

4. Are some members of your group better facial communicators (encoders) than others? Are some better receivers (decoders) than others? Is there a sex difference in the ability to encode? In the ability to decode? How might you account for the differences in these abilities?

## 3.2 Rules of Facial and Eye Communication

Identify three rules of *facial and eye movement* that differ for men and for women. [Note: rules may be conceived of as prescriptive (indicating what should be done) or as proscriptive (indicating what should not be done).]

1.

2.

3.

Identify three rules of *facial and eye communication* that may be useful in making contact (object: romance) with another person. In your statement of the rule be sure to indicate who is to serve as the "source" and who is to serve as the intended "receiver."

1.

2.

3.

Review the six rules you have identified and respond to the following:

1. What do these rules tell us about gender expectations and gender roles in our society?

2. Do you think these rules are changing? In what direction are they changing? Why are(n't) they changing?

3. Do you think these rules are cross-cultural or culture-specific? If possible, give examples of these same rules or contradictory rules from other cultures.

## 3.3   The Effects of Eye Contact

Form dyads and talk about any topic of mutual interest — sports, film, politics. For the first two minutes, the conversation should be conducted without any special rules. At an agreed-upon signal, eye-face contact is to cease. The conversation should continue for another two minutes as before, ideally without interruption. At another signal, focused eye-eye contact is to be established. Each person is to maintain direct eye contact for two minutes and continue the conversation as usual. At another signal, the participants should return to their customary means of communication for the final two minutes. Each person should share her or his feelings during the four periods:

1. normal interaction situation
2. no eye-contact situation
3. focused eye contact
4. normal situation but with heightened awareness and perhaps some awkwardness carried over from the two periods of abnormal interaction.

Specifically, members may address themselves to the influence of changes in eye contact on such variables as:

1. fluency, nonfluencies, and silences
2. general body movements, especially of head, hands, and legs
3. comfort or discomfort
4. interest in the other person and in the conversation.
5. time perception (did some eye-contact situations seem longer than others?)

What suggestions for effective interpersonal interaction might we derive from this brief experience?

## 3.4 Right and Left Movers*

Dyads should be formed. One person is designated A and the other B. For Round One, person A will be the observer and person B will be the observed. Person A should read the following questions to Person B and observe B's facial and eye responses as closely as possible. Person B should respond to these questions by figuring out the answers in his or her head.

**Round One.    Questions for Person B as read by Person A:**

1. How much is 18 × 6?

2. How many letters are there in the word *Washington*?

3. What does it mean to say: "Beauty is in the eye of the beholder?"

**Round Two. Questions for Person A as read by Person B:**

1. How much is 12 × 13?

2. How many letters are there in the word *generation*?

3. What does it mean to say: "It is better to have loved and lost than never to have loved at all"?

### Discussion

1. It has been found that approximately 75% of a person's eye movements will be made in the same direction, either to the left or to the right. In what direction did each person's eyes move in answering the questions?

2. Some researchers have suggested that right movers are using their left hemisphere to process information whereas left movers are using their right hemisphere. Several differences between left and right movers have been found and are summarized by Mark Knapp. Left movers are more susceptible to hypnosis, have more alpha brain waves, score higher on verbal SATs, have greater fluency in writing, have greater visual imagery, are more likely to major in the humanities, and are more sociable. Right movers, on the other hand, are more likely to show tension in large muscles, score higher on quantitative SATs, are more likely to major in the sciences, have more "tics" and "twitches," prefer "cool" colors, and make their career choices earlier. Do you find support for these findings in your own behaviors?

*This exercise is modeled on the research conducted by D. Galin and R. Ornstein, "Individual Differences in Cognitive Style. I. Reflective Eye Movements," *Neuropsychologia* 12 (1974): 367-376.

# 3.5  Observational Record of Facial and Eye Communication

This observational record form is designed to increase your awareness of the forms and functions of facial and eye communication and their role in the total communication act. For each example of facial and eye communication noted, (1) describe the specific manifestation of that communication, and indicate (2) the sources and receivers of the message; (3) the specific context in which the communication occurred; (4) the message or meanings that were communicated; (5) the effects of the nonverbal communication; and (6) any additional comments or questions that you feel are relevant to understanding the specific communication.

Affect display:

Eye contact:

Gaze:

Mutual gaze:

Pupil dilation:

Pupil constriction:


Left moving:


Right moving:


Other directed gaze:


Gaze aversion:


Winking:


Civil inattention:


Eye adornment:

# Review and Discussion Questions

1. It has been claimed that facial and eye cues are the most important of all nonverbal cues. Do you find evidence to support this assumption from your own experience in making inferences and in having inferences made about you?

2. How do you communicate the following with your face and eyes:
   a. romantic interest in another person
   b. a total lack of romantic interest in another person
   c. confidence
   d. happiness
   e. surprise

3. Of the facial management techniques considered in this chapter, which do you find particularly difficult? Particularly easy?

4. Can you identify yourself and others you know in terms of the styles of facial expression discussed in this chapter? Ask a few people who know you well if they can identify your style of facial expression. What can you do to change if you are not satisfied with the characterizations?

5. Examine four or five advertisements in which the face and eyes are prominently featured. What do the model's eye and facial expressions communicate? Identify the specific nonverbals that led to your conclusions.

6. How are eye and facial movements used in initial encounters? That is, how do people use their eyes and faces to communicate their interest or lack of interest in another person in the initial encounter?

# Terms to Define

Affect displays

Micromomentary expressions

Facial management techniques

Intensifying

Deintensifying

Neutralizing

Masking

Styles in facial expression

Eye contact

Eye avoidance

Civil inattention

Pupillometrics

Pupil dilation

Pupil constriction

Left movers

Right movers

Additional relevant terms in facial and eye communication

# 4
# Artifactual Communication

## Chapter Outline

## Objectives

After completing this chapter, you should be able to:

1. identify the general role of clothing in impression formation
2. provide examples of how clothing may communicate information about status, occupation, social awareness, and inner feelings
3. explain some of the messages that jewelry may communicate
4. explain the nature of color symbolism

Artifactual communication covers that broad area of nonverbal communication which includes communication through the selection and arrangement of objects. Clothing, jewelry, hair styles and the ways in which we adorn our own bodies are major examples of this type of nonverbal communication. In addition, the objects we have in our homes—oil paintings, posters, glass tables, oak chairs, antique furnishings—and their arrangement communicate a great deal about us. The colors we select for our homes, offices, and our clothing are similarly carriers of significant messages.

**Artifacts include the manipulation of objects in contact with the interacting persons which may act as nonverbal stimuli. These artifacts include perfume, clothes, lipstick, eyeglasses, wigs and other hairpieces, false eyelashes, eyeliners, and the whole repertoire of falsies and "beauty" aids.**

**Knapp, p. 19**

# Clothing Impressions

Consider, for example, the different impressions that clothing may communicate. The man's three piece pin-striped suit, white shirt, and yellow (with blue dots) tie communicate conformity to the rules of

---

*For thousands of years human beings have communicated with one another first in the language of clothes.*

Lurie, p. 3

---

many large corporations and signal that this particular man is both conscientious and ambitious. Consider the same man in jeans, a sweat shirt, and sneakers. Here he communicates a youthful spirit, an active (perhaps athletic) orientation, and casualness. Of course, each person's impressions of these two hypothetical men will differ in specifics but these meanings should seem reasonable if not complete. Even greater differences in impressions would probably result from similarly contrasting women. For example, consider the woman in the dark blue suit, white blouse, and high heels versus this same woman in jeans, a sweater, and sneakers. Again, we would probably form very different impressions of these two women. Though you and I may not necessarily agree on the specific meanings that the clothing communicates, we would probably agree that the two outfits will lead to drastically different impressions.

We learn to form impressions of people on the basis of their clothing early in life. For example, in one study children in the fourth and sixth grades were asked to rate the wearers of a variety of different types of jeans on the basis of popularity, attractiveness, and friendliness. Three types of jeans were used in the study: designer type and high priced (Calvin Klein), medium priced (Levi Strauss), and low priced (Sears Toughskins). The children rated the wearers of Levi Strauss jeans most favorably and the wearers of Sears jeans least favorably.

# The Messages of Clothing

Consider the clothes you are now wearing. What messages do these communicate? Do they say you are in style? Out of style? Wealthy? Poor? Do they communicate a sense of modesty? A sense of sensuousness? Do they communicate a particular mood? Do they communicate friendliness? Snobbishness? Clothing can communicate a wide variety of messages; here are a few.

## Status

Throughout history, clothes have been used to signal status. For example, in ancient Egypt only those of high status were allowed to wear sandals. Today, clothing still indicates status though in more subtle ways. Designer styling, expensive materials, and exactly-the-right clothing for exactly-the-right occasion all communicate high status. Off-the-rack, all-purpose, synthetics, on the other hand, communicate low status.

Similarly, low status is communicated generally (there are exceptions here) by "trendiness" whereas high status is communicated by a more conservative appearance.

## Occupation

Our clothing often signals our occupation. Obvious examples are uniforms worn by police officers, doctors and nurses, military personnel, the clergy, and sanitation workers. But there are other kinds of uniforms that, although we do not call them uniforms serve much the same function, namely to identify the occupation of the individual. For example, in many colleges only the male faculty wear jackets and ties. The famous "IBM Uniform" of dark suit and white shirt or blouse is another example.

It is interesting to note that although we do not have laws prohibiting people from wearing certain articles denoting high status, we do have laws prohibiting the wearing of certain uniforms. For example, it would be illegal for me to wear the uniform of a police officer or Army general.

## Social Awareness, Social Consciousness

Our clothing also communicates our awareness or our lack of awareness of the unwritten but rigidly enforced rules of society. Thus, to show up at a formal dinner in tennis sneakers and shorts would communicate a clear and obvious lack of social awareness. But, consider the messages that might be communicated by the man working in a conservative brokerage house who wears his hair down to his shoulders or the woman working as a social worker in a poor neighborhood who wears expensive jewelry. Consider, too, the messages communicated by those who wear wild animal furs.

> To choose clothes, either in a store or at home, is to define and
> describe outselves.
>
> Lurie, p. 5

## Inner Feelings

Clothing is an extremely personal thing and reflects our inner feelings probably more than we realize. When we are happy we probably wear clothes that are brighter than when we are sad. Similarly, when we are in good spirits, we probably give much greater attention to the way we dress than when we are depressed or lonely.

Further, clothing probably also influences the way we feel. For example, if we dress in dark, poorly-fitting, and generally unattractive clothes, we will probably feel more negatively than if we had dressed in bright, well-fitting, and attractive clothes. There are at least two reasons for this. First, through the meanings derived from association—in our selecting certain clothes and colors to reflect our moods and feelings, the clothes have come to mean certain things to us—our clothes now come to create these meanings as well as merely reflect them. Second, other people respond to us, at least in part, on the basis of how we look. When we look pleasant, others are more likely to respond to us pleasantly; when we look unpleasant, others are more likely to respond unpleasantly.

# Jewelry

Consider jewelry. Contrast the man who wears a ''simple'' Rolex watch and a wedding band with the man who wears three heavy gold chains (clearly displayed through a shirt opened almost to the navel), two bracelets, four extra large rings, and a watch with a thick gold bracelet and rhinestones for numbers. Again, we may not agree on the specific meanings that the different jewelry would communicate, but we would no doubt agree that the two men will be perceived very differently by most people. The same would hold true for the man with short hair versus the man with hair down to his shoulders.

Women are allowed a great deal more freedom in this area. It is not as easy to differentiate the woman with little jewelry from the woman with lots of jewelry. And certainly, we would be hard pressed to stereotype the woman with long hair and distinguish her from the woman with short hair. Hair length for women does not carry the same amount of information that it does for a man.

# Color

Perhaps the most obvious dimension of artifactual communication is color—the colors of our clothing, our homes, our offices and the colors of schools, hospitals, restaurants and other public places.

## Color Symbolism

Throughout history, different colors have been symbolic of different meanings. For example, red has been associated both with warmth, passion, life, liberty, and patriotism, and with death, war, revolution, the devil, and danger. Green is symbolic of nature, hope, freshness, and prosperity but also of envy, jealousy, opposition, and disgrace. Purple is the color of power and royalty in addition to mourning, regret, and penitence. Yellow is the color of wisdom and divinity as well as cowardice and malevolence.

The symbolism for colors is, of course, a cultural phenomenon. Each culture seems to have somewhat different meanings for each of the colors. For example, red in China is symbolic of joyous and festive occasions but in Japan symbolizes anger and danger. Green symbolizes femininity to certain American Indians, strength and fertility to Egyptians, and energy and youth to the Japanese.

In English, our connotative meanings for different colors vary considerably. For example, if you were asked to rank order yellow, green, red, gray, and blue in terms of general evaluation, that is, how good or bad each color is perceived, how would you rank them? You may wish to rank these before reading on. Most English speakers would rank them as follows, from best to worst: red and blue (about equally good), green, yellow, and gray. How would you rank these same colors in terms of their perceived strength or potency? Most English speakers would rank them as follows, from most potent to least potent: red, blue, green, yellow, and gray.

There is some evidence to show that different colors affect us physiologically in different ways. For example, red light seems to increase our respiratory movements while blue light seems to decrease them. This seems consistent with our intuitions about these two colors; blue seems soothing while red seems volatile. Schools and hospitals are painted pale colors (institutional green or tan, usually) in order to promote calm and relaxed feelings. Fast-food restaurants and many stores are painted bright colors to promote activity and raise energy levels.

## Color and Personality

Currently there is popular interest in the relationship between color preferences and personality. The popularity of these works seems to rest, at least in part, on the intuitive feelings we all have about the relationship between a person's color preferences—in, say, their clothes—and their personality. Outgoing people, for example, do seem to wear brighter colors than do introverts. Conservative people do seem to wear darker and more muted colors than do their more liberal counterparts. These, of course, are general feelings that we develop on the basis of our observations of others and, of course, these connections would change with the society and with the times.

Some researchers, however, have gone much further and offer detailed personality diagnoses based solely on color preferences. In *The Luscher Color Test*, for example, you are asked to indicate color likes and dislikes to a variety of colored squares and on the basis of these preferences, a personality profile is obtained.

In his *Color in Your World*, Faber Birren claims that if you like blue you are probably conservative, deliberate, and introspective. You have your own passions under control and are sensitive to the feelings of others. You are cautious in your communications, and your opinions and beliefs seldom change. You question everything you do not understand. If, on the other hand, you dislike blue then you are resentful of the success of others and may even take some joy in their failures. You feel unfulfilled in your emotional and intellectual lives. You are erratic and easily become irritated. This seems a great deal to derive from a simple liking or disliking for blue.

It is not surprising, therefore, that little research has confirmed the conclusions connecting color preferences and personality. One major reason seems to be that our color preferences are influenced by a variety of factors—our early exposure to color, our past experiences with colors, our occupation, and our sense of style, to name just a few—as well as our personality.

# Artifactual Communication Exercises

The exercises in this unit focus on increasing our understanding of the way in which objects and their arrangements communicate messages. The first exercise contains a questionnaire used in a study on the relationship between clothing preferences and personality. You may wish to complete *Clothing Questionnaire* so that you may further explore your own clothing preferences. In *Appearance and Status,* we examine some of the status symbols of our society that often go unnoticed (at least consciously).

The ways in which stores use artifactual communication to convey different images is explored in *Nonverbal Communication in the Stores.* The role of color in communication is explored in *Messages of Color* and *Color Symbolism.*

In *Clothing Consulting* you are asked to put your knowledge of artifactual communication to work and to make specific recommendations on how two individuals should dress. Again, applying your knowledge, you are asked—in *Aesthetic and Color Communication*—to suggest redesign plans for your classroom so that more effective teaching and learning may take place. Last, a form for recording observations is included, *Observational Record of Artifactual Communication.*

# 4.1  Clothing Questionnaire*

**Instructions:**

Indicate the extent to which each of the following statements accurately or inaccurately reflects your clothing preferences. Use the following scale:

5 = very accurate

4 = fairly accurate

3 = neither accurate, nor inaccurate

2 = fairly inaccurate

1 = very inaccurate

_____  1. I like close-fitting, figure-revealing clothes.

_____  2. I approve of skimpy bathing suits and wouldn't mind wearing one myself.

_____  3. I like to "dress up," and I usually spend a lot of time doing so.

_____  4. I usually dress for warmth rather than for fashion.

_____  5. When buying clothes, I am more interested in practicality than beauty.

_____  6. I see nothing wrong with wearing clothes which reveal a lot of skin.

_____  7. The people whom I know always notice what I wear.

_____  8. It is very important to be in style.

_____  9. There is nothing like a new article of clothing to improve my morale.

_____ 10. (Women) I think that most men "notice" what a woman is wearing.

_____     (Men) I think most women "notice" what a man is wearing.

_____ 11. I like to try out new "effects" in my clothing which others will admire and envy.

_____ 12. I buy clothes for comfort rather than appearance.

_____ 13. If I had more money I would spend it on clothes.

_____ 14. I should love to be a clothes designer.

_____ 15. I would love to be a clothes model.

_____ 16. I spend quite a bit of time reading about styles and fashions in magazines and newspapers.

_____ 17. I like clothes with bold designs.

**Scoring:** This questionnaire measures four dimensions of personality as revealed in your clothing preferences: clothing consciousness, exhibitionism, practicality, and designer leanings.

To compute your "clothing consciousness" score, add your responses for items 3, 7, 8, 9, 10, 11, 13, and 16. Your score should be somewhere between 8 and 40.

To compute your "exhibitionism" score, add your responses for items 1, 2, 6, and 17. Your score should be somewhere between 4 and 20.

To compute your "practicality" score, add your responses for items 4, 5, and 12. Your score should be somewhere between 3 and 15.

To compute your "designer leanings" score, add your responses for items 14 and 15. Your score should be somewhere between 2 and 10.

**What Your Scores Mean**

This clothing preferences questionnaire was designed by communication researchers to investigate the relationship between clothing behavior or preferences and a variety of personality variables. The researchers tried to discover if people who had the same clothing preferences were also similar on a variety of personality measures and if those who had very different clothing preferences were also different in terms of personality. Another way of putting this would be to ask: To what extent can we make predictions about an individual's personality on the basis of his or her clothing preferences? In order to answer that question the researchers correlated the results of the clothing preference questionnaire with a wide variety of personality tests, for example, the California Psychological Inventory; Edwards Personality Preference Schedule; Allport, Vernon, and Lindzey's Study of Values; the Tennessee Self-concept Scale, the Radicalism-conservatism scale, and a number of others. In all, 53 personality factors were investigated. The results presented here, then, are based on these extensive tests. Here is what your scores mean for each of the four dimensions measured:

**Clothing Consciousness**

High males (those with scores ranging from 32 to 40) are generally conforming. They do not value beauty and believe that people can be easily manipulated and, in fact, believe that clothing is a means for manipulating others. They are deliberate, guarded, and differential to authority, custom, and tradition.

In contrast, low males (those with scores ranging from 8 to 16) are generally aggressive, independent, adventurous, and outgoing. They are dependable and do not believe that people are easily manipulated.

High females (those with scores ranging from 32 to 40) were generally inhibited, loyal, anxious, kind, sympathetic, and loyal to friends. Like the high males, these females are also conforming.

Low females (those with scores ranging from 8 to 16) are forceful, dominant, clear thinking. Like the low males these women are independent and do not believe that people are easily manipulated.

## Exhibitionism

High males (those with scores ranging from 16 to 20) are aggressive, confident, unsympathetic, have low family self-concepts, moody, and unaffectionate. They are generally outgoing and are often impulsive.

Low males (those with scores ranging from 4 to 8) are generally guarded about revealing things about themselves; they are low self-disclosers. They believe people are easily manipulated but do not believe that exhibitionism is appropriate. They have high self-concepts regarding their families.

High females (those with scores ranging from 16 to 20) are radical, have high moral and ethical self-concepts, and are generally detached in their relationships.

Low females (those with scores ranging from 4 to 8) are timid, with feelings of inferiority. They have low motivation for heterosexual relationships, are sincere, accepting of others, and patient.

## Practicality

High males (those with scores ranging from 12 to 15) are generally inhibited and are not leadership oriented. They are rebellious, cautious, and generally dissatisfied. They have a low motivation for establishing friendship relationships.

Low males (those with scores ranging from 3 to 6) are success oriented, forceful, mature, and serious.

High females (those with scores ranging from 12 to 15) are clever, enthusiastic, guarded, confident (in fact, have feelings of superiority), and outgoing. Despite their feelings of superiority, they are not oriented to leadership positions.

Low females (those with scores ranging from 3 to 6) are self-centered and independent. Like their male counterparts, they are not oriented to the establishment of friendship relationships.

## Designer Leanings

High males (those with scores ranging from 8 to 10) are cooperative, warm, impulsive, irritable, sympathetic, helpful, demanding, and worry considerably about their behavior.

Low males (those with scores ranging from 2 to 4) are adventurous, egotistical (with feelings of superiority), independent, anxious, and generally dissatisfied. They are generally not interested in forming friendship relationships.

High females (those with scores ranging from 8 to 10) are generally irrational, confused, uncritical, quick, and expressive.

Low females (those with scores ranging from 2 to 4) are generally efficient, clear thinking, resourceful, but disorganized under pressure.

**Discussion:**

[The scoring procedure and the scores defining high and low ratings were not used in the original study but are used here to simplify the questionnaire's use in a nonverbal communication course.]

In groups of five or six discuss this questionnaire and your individual results. Consider some or all of the following:

1. How accurate do you think these findings are? What evidence can you offer to support your position?

2. What other factors might be correlated with your clothing preferences? In what way?

3. How might your clothing communicate to yourself? That is, does the clothing you wear influence your attitudes and behaviors? Do you, for example, function differently when wearing drastically different attire? Explain.

4. What do your instructor's clothing preferences lead you to think about him or her? How accurate do you think you are?

*[This questionnaire and the research findings are from L. B. Rosenfeld and T. G. Plax, "Clothing as Communication," *Journal of Communication* 27 (1977): 23-31. Reprinted by permission of Lawrence Rosenfeld and Lewis Aiken, on whose work Rosenfeld based his questionnaire.]

# 4.2   Appearance and Status

**Directions:**

For each of the items listed below, indicate the social class status that it most probably communicates or reveals. For convenience, use the following distinctions and abbreviations:

U = Upper status (lots of money, high social position)

M = Middle status (financially comfortable, in high status positions)

L = Lower status (not much money, blue collar jobs or no jobs at all)

O = Makes no reference to social status

_____ attractiveness (handsome men and beautiful women)

_____ lots of smiling

_____ hair in latest style on female

_____ hair piece on male

_____ wool, leather, silk, cotton, fur

_____ synthetic fibers (especially polyester)

_____ legible clothing (clothing with writing on it)

_____ attaché case

_____ vest over a T-shirt

_____ Cartier tank watch

_____ Timex watch

_____ 20-function, digital, calculator watch

_____ dark silk necktie with small white dots

_____ black raincoat for male

_____ top brand liquor

**Answers:**

Here are the "answers" to the Appearance and Status exercise. These "answers" are intended more to stimulate discussion than to provide definitive conclusions about the status communicated by any given object or article of clothing. In considering these "answers" try to think of reasons why a status other than that listed would also be a logical choice. These examples and much of the reasoning used here were taken from Paul Fussell's entertaining and insightful *Class: A Guide Through the American Status System* (New York: Summit, 1983). Another helpful guide in this area is John Molloy's *Molloy's Live for Success* (New York: Bantam, 1981). These works will prove especially helpful in clarifying the status messages that clothing and a wide variety of other artifacts communicate.

**Attractiveness: U**

The idea here is that attractiveness is used to raise one's social status. Attractive people are more likely to marry into money and social position than are unattractive people. As a result, the upper social class will have an inordinate number of attractive people entering into it.

**Smiling: L or M**

Generally we find that the lower and middle classes smile a great deal more than the upper classes. Perhaps the idea here is that smiling is used as a means of ingratiating oneself with others. This need is greatest in the lower and middle classes and least in the upper classes.

**Hair in Latest Style: M**

The middle classes have the strongest need to be in style. The lower classes do not have the money and the upper classes are too concerned with other issues to worry about hair styles.

**Hair Piece on Male: M**

As with the latest hair style, a hairpiece is designed to gain acceptance, to look better than one might otherwise look. The upper classes have little need for this; their status speaks for who they are. The lower classes either cannot afford hairpieces or do not care enough about appearance. Their money and their energies are better put to other ends. The middle class, concerned as it is with acceptance, will generally devote the most attention to appearance.

**Wool, Leather, Silk, Cotton, Fur: U**
**Synthetic Fibers: L**

Organic materials are generally the most expensive and hence would be bought most by the upper classes. Synthetic fibers (especially polyester) are relatively inexpensive and are easiest to care for (for example, we can hand wash them) and hence are the logical fabric of the lower classes. The middle classes would attempt to emulate the upper classes and would be more likely to buy organic materials.

**Legible Clothing: M or L**

If the writing is sophisticated (for example, shirts with Mozart or PBS or *The New Yorker* on them) then the wearer may be middle class. If the writing is gross or humorous, the wearer is probably lower class. Labels such as Gucci, Louis Vitton, and Cartier would generally signal upper class while labels such as Guess, Members Only, and the like would signal middle or upper lower classes.

**Attaché Case: M**

This is the symbol par excellence of the middle class. It represents upward movement. Upper class members do not have a need for such outward signs of upward mobility; they are already "up." The lower classes are too far from the occupations that require or cultivate attaché carrying.

**Vest Over T-Shirt: L**

This is the symbol for all "Ed Nortons," the blue collar workers and those without jobs.

**Cartier Tank Watch: U**
**Timex Watch: L or U**
**20-Function, Digital, Calculator Watch: M**

Watches are especially good status indicators. Generally, the simpler and the more expensive the watch the higher the status. Thus, the Cartier tank watch or the Rolex are especially clear symbols of the upper class. The Timex, on the other hand, in being purely functional may also be used by the upper classes who have nothing to gain by flaunting a prestigious watch. The Timex, however, would also be used by the lower classes because it is so inexpensive. The middle class, although they may emulate the upper classes and buy a high status watch, often select a watch that is somewhat more ostentatious, for example, the watch with twenty different functions, four different push buttons, a calculator, and the like.

**Dark Silk Nectie: U or M**

This tie has the highest status. It is the most expensive and, for some reason, has been accorded a high status position.

### Black Raincoat for Male: M

The high status color for a man's raincoat is tan. It gets dirty especially fast but rich people can afford to have it cleaned. Black raincoats do not show the dirt and do not need to be cleaned so often and consequently are good choices for the middle class. In fact, it is difficult to find a black raincoat costing in the high price range for raincoats. Burberry raincoats, for example, which are high status raincoats, only come in tan.

### Top Brand Liquor: M

The middle class, in its desire for status and recognition, will pay extra for labels. In fact, they will often buy cheap brand liquor and pour it into expensively labeled bottles to create what they hope will be the right impression. The upper classes have no need for ''putting on the dog'' and will, as a result, probably buy average priced liquor. The lower classes, since they cannot afford the extra cost, will be content with the ''no frills'' varieties.

# 4.3 Nonverbal Communication in the Stores

The purpose of this exercise is to sensitize you to the ways and means that retail stores use to communicate a particular image and to provide some experience in analyzing artifactual communication. For this exercise two stores selling the same type of merchandize but differing greatly in the price of the items should be compared. Suitable stores for this exercise will depend, of course, on the specific city or community in which you are living. For example, in New York suitable stores might be the drug stores, Casswell-Massey and Duane Reade, Rite-Aide, or Pathmark; the department stores, Bloomingdales or Lord and Taylor or B. Altmans and K-Mart; the chocolate stores, Perugina, Godiva or Kron and Fanny Farmer or Barracini; and the jewelry stores, Cartier or Tiffanys and any local jewelry store.

Visit each of the stores and observe the differences between them on each of the following variables.

1. the space devoted to items for sale versus items that are decorative
2. the aisle space
3. the type, quality, and quantity of decorations
4. the sale signs and price signs—their size, prominence, color, and quantity
5. the lighting, its type (for example, ceiling or table lamps) and level (for example, high, medium, and low intensity)
6. the predominant color scheme
7. the personnel—age, sex, and dress especially
8. the behavior of the personnel
9. the type of flooring
10. the type of wall design (for example, mirror, tile, painted surfaces, wallpaper)
11. the materials used in displaying the merchandize (for example, wood cases, formica display tables, chrome and glass shelves)
12. the quantity of items displayed
13. the types of people shopping in the stores (for example, their age, dress, apparent status)
14. the window decorations
15. the store name (for example, its display outside the store, its display inside the store, the labels that bear the store name)

In addition, respond to the following:

1. Did you feel more comfortable in one store rather than in the other? Why?

2. In which store did you spend more time? Why? Did time seem to go faster in one store? Explain.

3. If you had to work in one of the stores, which one would you select? Why?

4. In which store did the customers move faster? Explain possible reasons for any differences noticed in the pace of the customers.

5. Which store would you be more likely to return to? Why?

After identifying the differences between these two stores, what generalizations might you offer for communicating different images? That is, how would you design a store if you wanted to sell high-priced items? How would you design a store if you wanted to sell low-priced items?

## 4.4 Messages of Color

The purpose of this exercise is to sensitize us to some of the messages communicated (or thought to be communicated) by various colors.

The class is broken down into seven groups; each group is assigned a specific color (blue, red, green, yellow, brown, white, and black are perhaps the easiest to work with). In order that each member of the group visualizes the same shade, paint chips or pictures illustrating a particular shade of the color should be used. Before any interaction among group members takes place, each person should individually complete the following questionnaire for the specific color assigned (noted here as "X").

**Color Questionnaire**

1. The personality of a person whose favorite color is X may best be described as

   _____ , _____ , and _____ .

2. The personality of a person who has an extreme dislike for X may best be described

   as _____ , _____ , and _____ .

3. When I visualize X, my thoughts and feelings can best be described as

   _____ , _____ , and _____ .

4. My first impression of a book whose cover is X is that the book is

   _____ .

5. My first impression of a man who wears X a great deal is that the man is

   _____ .

6. My first impression of a woman who wears X a great deal is that the woman is

   _____ .

7. Do certain colors appear masculine (or communicate masculinity in some way) and certain colors appear feminine (or communicate femininity in some way)? Which colors would you categorize as masculine? Why? Which colors would you categorize as feminine? Why?

8. My first impression of a room decorated in X is that the room is

   _____ .

9. What colors would you use to package the following products? Why?

   a.  A new and powerful detergent _____

   b.  An expensive line of chocolate chip cookies _____

   c.  An extremely powerful personal computer _____

   d.  A mild liquid laxative _____

   e.  An expensive gold watch _____

10. What colors would you use to communicate the following feelings and characteristics? Why?

   a.  Friendliness _____

   b.  Hostility _____

   c.  Warmth _____

   d.  Sex appeal _____

   e.  Love _____

   f.  Satisfaction _____

   g.  Anger _____

   h.  Strength _____

   i.  Weakness _____

   j.  Happiness _____

After all persons have filled out this brief questionnaire, group members should share their responses and attempt to derive some general statements concerning the messages that their color seems to communicate. When this is completed, all groups should compare their results, considering such issues as the following.

1. How much agreement or lack of it was evidenced in identifying the messages these colors communicate? Was there greater agreement for some colors than for others? Why?

2. How accurate do you think your inferences about personality and color preferences would be? How accurate do you think your first impressions of a book would be? Of men and women? Of a room?

3. How universal do you think the impressions that people get from various colors are? For example, do men and women get the same impressions on the basis of color? Would young and old derive the same impressions? Would members of different cultures? Explain.

4. In what ways is color important to the manufacturer and the advertiser? Are they successful in getting their message across to you? Explain.

# 4.5 Color Symbolism

Here is an opportunity for you to do some research into the reasons for color symbolism. Presented below are various colors and at least one symbol that each color represents.

1. Why is green the color of envy?

2. Why is white the color of purity?

3. Why is black or purple the color of mourning?

4. Why is blue the color for boys?

5. Why is pink the color for girls?

6. Why is yellow the color of cowardice?

7. Why is red (scarlet red) the color of adultry?

8. Why is purple the color of royalty?

9. Why does ''in the pink'' mean ''in good health''?

10. Why does "seeing red" mean "great anger"?

11. Why does "I'm blue" mean "I'm sad"?

12. Why are brown, red, and orange "warm" colors?

13. Why are green, indigo, and violet "cold" colors?

14. Why are purple and yellow the colors of Easter?

15. Why are green and red the colors of Christmas?

16. Why are orange and black the colors of Halloween?

17. Why does "true blue" mean "loyal"?

18. Why is green the color for "go"?

19. Why is red the color for "stop"?

20. Why is amber the color for "caution"?

# 4.6 Clothing Consulting

Because of your expertise in nonverbal communication you have been called to serve as a consultant for Jack and Jill. Using your knowledge of nonverbal communication, make recommendations on these several issues.

Jack and Jill have recently graduated from college as Economics majors with a concentration in Finance. They are interested in pursuing careers with a large and conservative brokerage house.

Advise both Jack and Jill how to dress for their first interview. Design their wardrobe in detail, including the types of clothes they should wear, the fabrics, and the colors of all major clothing items. They also wish to know:

a. What should they bring with them to help them make a favorable impression?

b. At what time should they arrive for their interview? (The interview is set for 1:00 p.m.)

(For questions c and d include any and all nonverbal behaviors that will be perceived by the interviewer.)

c. What nonverbal behaviors should they be certain to avoid? Why?

d. What nonverbal behaviors should they use to help them make the right impression? Why will these behaviors contribute to "the right impression"?

# 4.7  Aesthetic and Color Communication

The purpose of this exercise is to explore the influence that our physical environment has on interpersonal communication. Form groups of five or six at random. The task of each group is to redesign your classroom so that it is more conducive to the aims of this course. Allow 15 to 20 minutes for the groups to come up with a new design.

("Redesign" should be taken to mean anything that is possible to do within the rules or restrictions imposed by the school and would include changing, adding, or removing any materials that may and can be changed, added, or removed by the group.)

After each group has planned the "new" classroom, the designs should be shared with the other members of the class. From all the suggestions, a composite redesigned classroom should be constructed and put into actual operation for at least a week of classes.

Before this design is put into effect, discussion should cover at least the following areas:

1. In what ways will this new design facilitate interpersonal communication? Be as specific as possible.

2. How would the classroom be designed if a party were to be held in it? Why? A formal lecture? Why?

3. If you could paint the classroom any color(s) you wanted to, what color(s) would you select? Why?

# 4.8  Observational Record of Artifactual Communication

This observational record form is designed to increase your awareness of the forms and functions of artifactual communication and its role in the total communication act. For each example of artifactual communication noted, (1) describe the specific manifestation of that communication, and indicate (2) the sources and receivers of the message; (3) the specific context in which the communication occurred; (4) the message or meanings that were communicated; (5) the effects of the nonverbal communication; and (6) any additional comments or questions that you feel are relevant to understanding the specific communication.

Comfort-protection clothing:

Modesty clothing:

Cultural display clothing:

Cultural badge:

Artifacts:

Status Symbol:

# Review and Discussion Questions

1. Do you draw inferences about others from the clothing they wear? What do you look for in clothing that is particularly helpful in drawing such inferences? Are you generally correct? Incorrect? Do you draw inferences concerning the other person's status, occupation, social awareness, and inner feelings? What specific clothing cues do you use in making these inferences? What other meanings does clothing communicate?

2. What messages do you wish your present clothing to communicate? What other messages have you used clothing to communicate? Were you successful in communicating the desired meanings? Explain.

3. What inferences do you draw from jewelry?

4. What artifactual cues, present in your own living space, communicate your own status, age, sex, and occupation?

5. How do you use color in both sending and receiving messages?

6. Color symbolism abounds in our language: "green with envy," "in the pink," "talk a blue streak," and "paint the town red" are just a few. What other examples can you provide? Why do you suppose the specific color was used in the phrase?

7. How do advertisers use color to communicate their messages? Select a specific advertisement that uses color to communicate a specific message and explain why you think it is effective or ineffective.

8. Do you think a relationship exists between color preferences on the one hand and personality on the other? Explain.

# Terms to Define

Artifactual communication


Artifactual status messages


Artifactual occupational messages


Artifactual social-awareness, social-consciousness messages


Artifactual inner-feelings messages


Color symbolism


Additional relevant terms in artifactual communication

# 5

# Spatial Communication
## (Proxemics and Territoriality)

## Objectives

After completing this chapter, you should be able to:

1. define *proxemics*
2. explain the four major proxemic distances: intimate, personal, social, and public
3. identify at least four influences on the maintenance of proxemic distances
4. define and distinguish between *crowding* and *density*
5. define and provide examples of *surveillance, behavioral constraint,* and *stimulus overload*
6. define *territoriality*
7. define and distinguish among *primary territory, secondary territory,* and *public territory*
8. define *territorial encroachment* and its several forms: *violation, invasion,* and *contamination*
9. define and give examples of the four major reactions to territorial encroachment: *withdrawal, turf defense, insulation,* and *linguistic collusion*
10. define *marker* and distinguish among the three main types: *central, boundary,* and *ear markers*

In this chapter we focus on spatial communication. Generally, we distinguish two areas concerned with space: proxemics and territoriality.

# Proxemics

*Proxemics,* a term coined by anthropologist Edward T. Hall, refers to the communicative function of space, for example, the way in which we use space in our interactions with others and what these different distances communicate and how they influence communication; the layout of our homes, offices, prisons, hospitals, and schools; and even the layout of our towns and cities.

> [Proxemics is] the study of man's perception and use of space.
>
> Edward T. Hall, "Proxemics,"
> Current Anthropology 9
> (1968), p. 83

# Proxemic Distances

Perhaps the most important dimension of proxemics is the different distances that we maintain when we communicate. Hall, for example, has identified four major proxemic distances which correspond to the four types of interactions we have with others.

## Intimate Distance

Intimate distance ranges from actual touching, in its close phase, to maintaining a distance of 6 to 18 inches, in its far phase. In this distance the presence of the other individual is clear and unmistakable. At the intimate distance we can touch, caress, and hold the other person; we can smell the other person's breath and body odor.

---

**Proxemics is the study of the use of space. Messages ranging from status to liking are communicated through the use of space; they vary according to factors such as sex, age, circumstances, and other nonverbal dimensions such as eye contact, body posture, and facial expression.**

**Malandro and Barker, p. 213**

---

## Personal Distance

Personal distance ranges from 1.5 to 2.5 feet in its close phase to 2.5 to 4 feet in its far phase. In the close phase we can still touch the other person but only by extending our arms. In the far phase touching is possible only if both individuals extend their arms.

## Social Distance

Social distance ranges from 4 to 7 feet in its close phase to 7 to 12 feet in its far phase. Business transactions take on a more formal tone if held at this distance. Eye contact is essential at this distance if communication is to take place. When there is not enough space to maintain social distance and yet that is the distance desired, then we make various adjustments such as arranging the furniture so that the desks, for example, face in different directions.

## Public Distance

Public distance ranges from 12 to 15 feet in its close phase to 25 feet and over in its far phase. At this distance we can easily take defensive action should that be necessary. This is the distance, therefore, that we might keep from a drunkard.

## Proxemic Influences

The distance that we maintain between ourselves and others is influenced by a variety of factors. For example, people of equal status usually maintain closer distances that do people of very different status levels. The culture in which we were raised will also exert an influence. Mediterranean cultures—Italian, Spanish, French, and Greek, for example—maintain closer distances than do Americans and most northern Europeans. Women generally maintain closer distances than do men, and children maintain closer distances than do adults. Generally, we maintain closer distances with those we like than with those we dislike.

# Crowding and Privacy

One of the most important dimensions of space is the degree of crowding or privacy that we experience. We seem to have needs that extend in both directions; we need to be one of the crowd, to feel a part of the happenings around us. At the same time, however, we have a need for privacy, to be removed from the crowd.

Crowding is a psychological perception that there are too many people around and we become conscious of restrictions on our spatial freedom. Crowding is clearly subjective. Two persons in the exact same situation may develop very different perceptions; one may feel crowded and restricted and one may feel totally free of any restrictions. Density, on the other hand, is a term used to refer objectively to the number of persons in a particular area of space. Thus, when we speak of the density of different cities we are referring to the number of people within each of the cities. When we speak of the crowding of different cities we are referring to the feelings that people feel restricted.

Nonverbal researchers identify three factors that contribute to a person's discomfort, to a persons' perception of being crowded: surveillance, behavioral constraint, and stimulus overload.

## Surveillance

When we feel we are being watched, particularly by strangers, we feel crowded. Their eyes intrude on our personal space and thus we feel restrictions on our own behaviors.

## Behavioral Constraint

When there are restrictions on our freedom of movement, we feel crowded. In a highly dense subway car in New York City, for example, there are great restrictions on our freedom of movement and so we perceive crowding.

## Stimulus Overload

When the visual and auditory stimuli around us become greater than we can effectively deal with, we have a case of stimulus overload. In such a case, we would perceive crowding much more readily than we would if this level of stimuli was more manageable.

We know that animals, when placed in high density environments will engage in bizarre behaviors. For example, they become aggressive, will attack those with whom they would normally live peacefully under less dense conditions, and will no longer care for and feed their young.

In studies of density and crowding in prisons, it has been found that the death rate for prisoners was ''conservatively two to one higher'' during high density times than during low density times. Similarly, blood pressure levels were found to be higher for inmates having an average of 19 square feet in their cells than for inmates having an average of 29 square feet.

The implications of research on spatial needs and responses to high density and crowding are only just beginning to be incorporated into the construction of housing, prisons, and hospitals. Hopefully, we will find here a significant practical application for these intriguing research findings.

## Privacy

Privacy may be seen as the other end of the spectrum. Privacy is perceived when we are free to move about as we wish, free from the eyes of others, and when our senses can easily deal with the stimuli around us. Put differently, privacy may be seen as freedom from surveillance, behavioral constraint, and stimulus overload.

At one extreme we might visualize the rich and powerful who have huge homes and surrounding lands to ensure their privacy. At the other extreme, are the poor who live in cramped quarters or prisoners who live in 6 by 9 cells under constant surveillance with extreme constraints on their behavior. In the last example, the prisoners probably experience severe stimulus overload occasioned by the lack of partitions between cells and the "open" walls separating walkways from living quarters.

---

**Territoriality is usually defined as a set of behaviors by which an organism characteristically lays claim to an area, demarcates it, and defends it against members of its own species.**

**Fried and DeFazio, in Katz and Katz, p. 27**

---

# Territoriality

*Territoriality*, a term that comes to us from ethology (the study of animals in their natural habitat) refers to the ownership- like reaction to a particular space. The actual spaces for which one might develop a territorial reaction range widely and would include one's country, home, kitchen, easy chair, and desk at the office or at school.

Irwin Altman, in his influential *The Environment and Social Behavior*, distinguishes three kinds of territories: primary, secondary, and public.

## Primary Territory

Primary territory refers to those areas which we might call ours. These territories are our exclusive preserve. Your room or apartment or house, your desk, your briefcase are all examples of primary territory. It is interesting to note that our power is generally increased when we are in our primary territory. For example, if two executives of the same status meet to discuss an issue, it is likely that the executive in whose office the meeting takes place will have the greater power.

## Secondary Territory

Secondary territory refers to those areas which are not our exclusive preserve and actually do not belong to us but which we have occupied for a length of time or have been associated with for one reason or another. One's neighborhood turf, a local bar that one frequents, or a table that one occupies with regularity in the school cafeteria are examples of secondary territories. We feel a definite ownership-like reaction to these territories and react negatively when "outsiders" attempt to occupy "our" territory.

## Public Territory

Public territory refers to areas that are technically open to all people. The beach, the movie house, and the college cafeteria are examples of public territories. Note, however, that even here we stake out and claim areas for our temporary use. Thus, for example, we lay out our beach towel, portable radio, and cooler in a way that communicates our "ownership" (even if temporary and illusory) of this particular piece of beach. Friends may enter but strangers may not.

# Territorial Encroachment

Frequently, one's territory is encroached upon by others. In *violation* there is unwarranted use of another's territory as when we enter another's office or home without permission. In *invasion* we enter the territory of another and by our invasion change the meaning of that territory, for example, the supervisor enters the meeting of the office staff and thereby changes the meaning of that territory. In *contamination* one renders the territory of another impure as when, for example, someone smokes a smelly cigar in a windowless office.

> The term *territoriality* has been used for years in the study of animal and fowl behavior. Generally, it has come to mean behavior characterized by identification with an area in such a way as to indicate ownership and defense of this territory against those who may "invade" it.
>
> Knapp, p. 115

## Reactions to Territorial Encroachment

When someone encroaches on our territory, we can react in a number of ways: withdrawal, turf defense, insulation, and linguistic collusion.

*Withdrawal* is the most obvious way; we can simply leave the scene—the country, the home, the office, the classroom. But we can also react by *turf defense*, that is, we can defend the territory against invaders. We can *insulate* ourselves by erecting some sort of barrier between ourselves and the invaders. We can also engage in *linguistic collusion*; that is, we can speak in a language or sublanguage that the invaders do not understand and thereby exclude them from interpersonal interaction.

# Markers

Whereas animals mark their territory by urinating, human use a wide variety of markers. *Central markers* are placed in a territory to reserve it for us. For example, we place a jacket over a chair or a book on a table to reserve it for us. *Boundary markers* divide our territory from that of another person. The arms rests in a theatre are good examples of boundary markers. *Ear markers*, a term that derives from the practice of branding animals on their ears, are marks that indicate that ownership of an object or space. Initials on an attaché case or a name plate on an office door would be examples of ear markers.

# Spatial Communication Exercises

The exercises in spatial communication are designed to enable you to work actively with some of the concepts in proxemics and territoriality. Opportunities to design classrooms and offices for different purposes are provided in *Environmental Design* and *Consulting about Space*. The ways in which we select seating positions based on our feelings about people and the communication functions to be fulfilled are covered in *Spatial Relationships and Communication Functions* and in *Interpersonal Interactions and Space*.

In *Theories about Space*, two theories about the way in which we treat space—*protection theory* and *equilibrium theory*—are defined briefly. The objective of this exercise is to design an observational study to test one or both of the theories. This exercise is a simplified version of the research study exercise presented in Appendix B and will serve as a useful preliminary for the later, more sophisticated and detailed research exercise. The *Observational Record of Spatial Communication* should enable you to increase your awareness of the forms and functions of space and territory in your own behaviors and in the total communication act.

# 5.1 Environmental Design

**Classroom Design**

1. Design a classroom for 30 students that will encourage student interaction and student-teacher informality and personalness. The classroom is 48 x 24 feet.

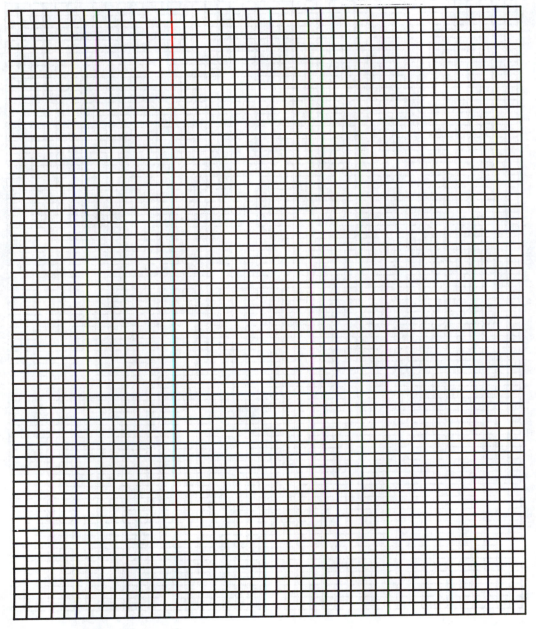

Each box equals one square foot.

2. Design a classroom for 30 students that will discourage student interaction and encourage an atmosphere of formality and impersonalness. The classroom is 48 x 24 feet.

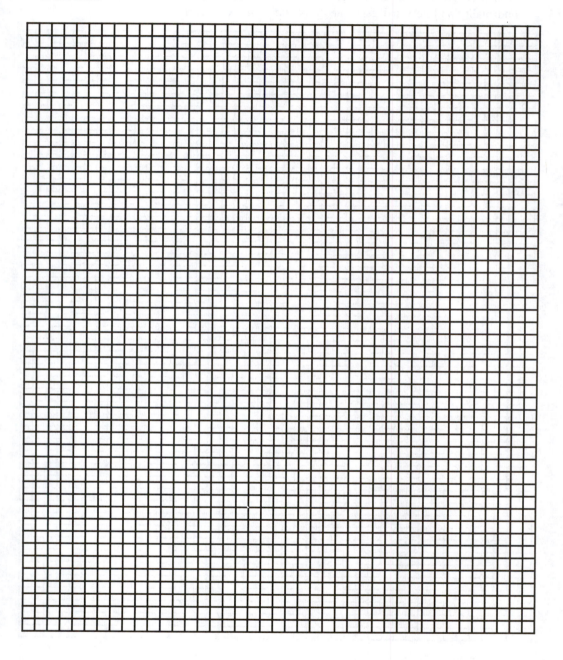

Each box equals one square foot.

**Office Design**

1. Design an office for four graduate assistants (all are of equal status) who want to be able to maintain privacy at certain times and at other times want to interact with each other in an informal atmosphere. This office is 24 x 24 feet.

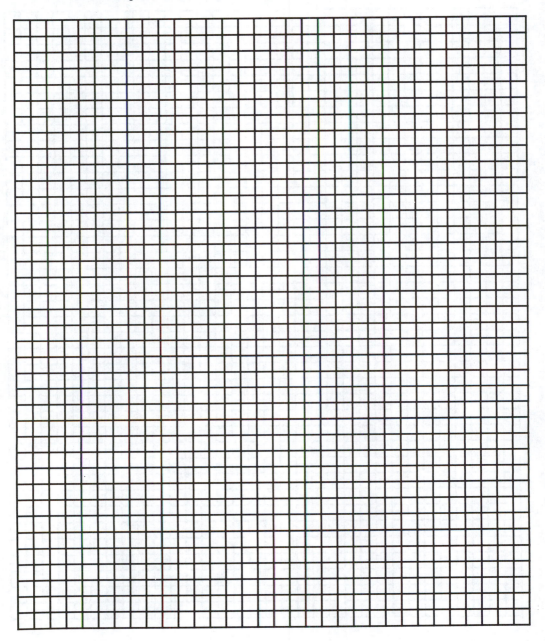

Each box equals one square foot.

2. Design an office for four persons: a manager who is in charge and who will maintain total decision-making authority and three assistants who will do the assignments the manager gives them. This particular manager is especially status conscious and wants the office to reflect the status differences. This office is 24 x 24 feet.

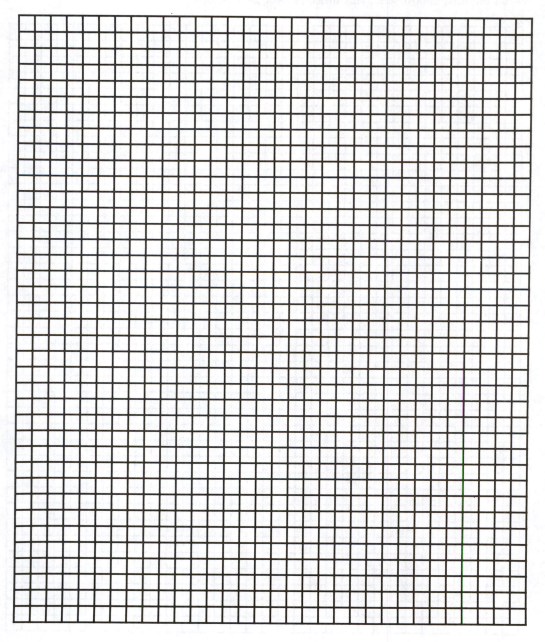

Each box equals one square foot.

## 5.2 Consulting About Space

Because of your expertise in nonverbal communication and especially in proxemics, you are called upon to offer advice as a nonverbal consultant on the following issues and problems.

1. Pat Bennington, an instructor at Utopia College, wants to encourage students to be more relaxed and more open when they come into the office to talk. How would you suggest that this instructor design the office so that students will feel relaxed, will be open in their discussions, and so that the general atmosphere is personal rather than impersonal. Absolute necessities are a desk, desk chair, three bookcases, and a four-drawer file cabinet. The office is 12 x 12 feet.

   Arrange these essential furnishings, select any other furnishings (money is no object), and select the colors you would use. Explain your design to the class in a short oral report or in a written paper. Explain too how your design will contribute to a relaxed, open, and informal atmosphere.

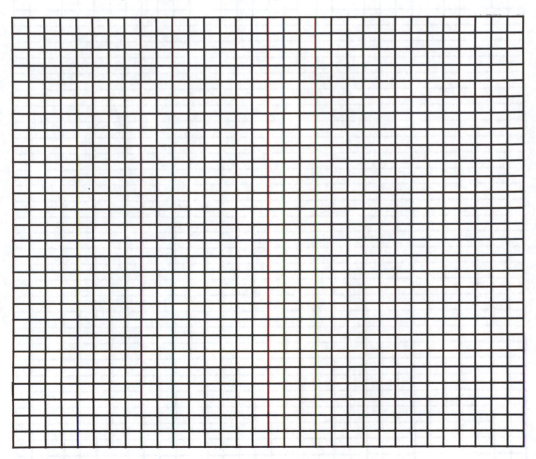

Each box equals one square foot.

2. Chris Wellington has recently risen from the ranks and now must exercise authority over former colleagues as a new vice-president. Although Chris and the four managers being supervised must all occupy the same space, the furnishings may be arranged in any way you suggest. Redesign the office to better meet the needs of the new vice-president. This office is 36 x 30 feet.

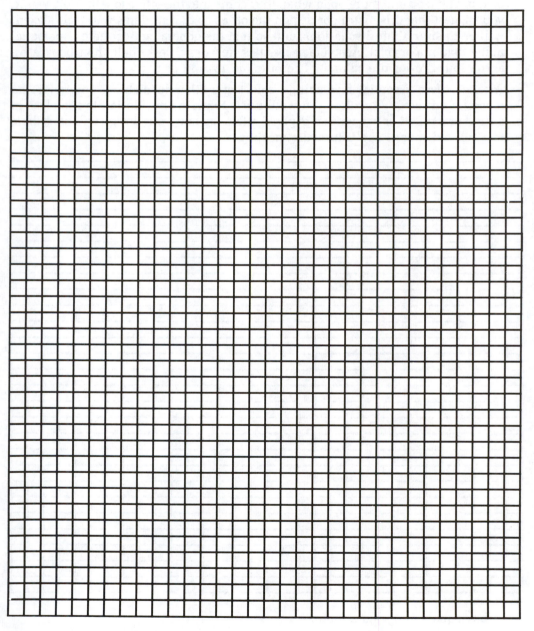

Each box equals one square foot.

3. The Real Estate Department of Louis Associates has the following personnel:

| | |
|---|---|
| Assistant One | Middle Manager One |
| Assistant Two | Middle Manager Two |
| Assistant Three | Middle Manager Three |
| Lower Level Manager One | Upper Manager One |
| Lower Level Manager Two | Upper Manager Two |
| Lower Level Manager Three | Upper Manager Three |

The following additional information is significant. Each of the Upper Managers requires approximately 50% of an assistant's time. Each Middle Manager requires approximately 30% of an assistant's time. Each Lower Level Manager requires approximately 20% of an assistant's time. Each assistant and each manager needs a desk, a desk chair, and a file cabinet.

Arrange this office to promote maximum efficiency and at the same time to reflect the status differences and similarities among the managers. This office is 48 x 48 feet.

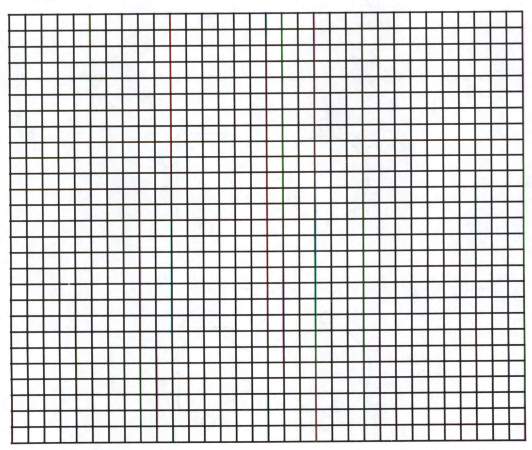

Each box equals two square feet.

# 5.3 Spatial Relationships and Communication Functions

Presented here are diagrams of tables and chairs. Imagine that the situation is the school cafeteria and that this is the only table not occupied. For each of the diagrams, place an X where you and a friend of the same sex would seat yourselves for each of the four conditions noted. Do this for *both* the round and the rectangular tables.

1. Conversing, for example, to talk for a few minutes before class

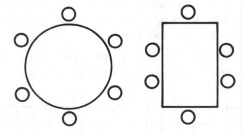

2. Cooperating, for example, to study together for the same exam or to work out a math problem

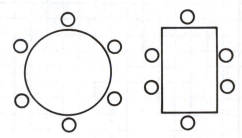

3. Coacting, for example, to study for different exams

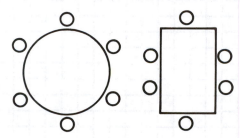

4. Competing, for example, to see who would be the first to solve a series of puzzles

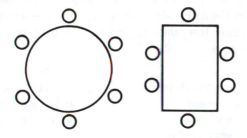

**For Discussion**

1. Why did you select the positions you did?

2. Explain the differences in the opportunity for nonverbal interaction that the different positions chosen allow.

3. How do these different positions relate to verbal communication?

4. Would you have chosen the same positions if you were romantically interested in the other person? Explain.

5. Compare your responses with the responses of others. How do you account for the differences in seating preferences?

6. Are there significant differences in choices between the round and the rectangular tables? Explain.

# 5.4   Interpersonal Interactions and Space

Presented here are diagrams of tables and chairs. Imagine that the situation is the school cafeteria and that this is the only table not occupied. In the space marked X is seated the person described above the diagram. Indicate by placing an X in the appropriate circle where you would sit.

1. A young man or woman to whom you are physically attracted and whom you would like to date but to whom you have never spoken

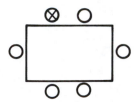

2. A person whom you find physically unattractive and to whom you have never spoken

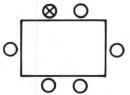

3. A person you dated once and had a miserable time with and whom you would never date again

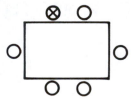

4. A person you have dated a few times and would like to date again

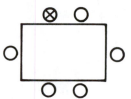

5. An instructor who gave you an undeserved F in a course last semester and whom you dislike intensely

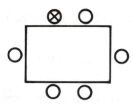

6. Your favorite instructor, whom you would like to get to know better

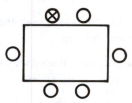

**For Discussion**

1.  Why did you select the positions you did? For example, how does the position you selected better enable you to achieve your purpose?

2.  Assume that you were already seated in the position marked X. Do you think that the person described would sit where you indicated you would (assuming that the feelings and motives are generally the same)? Why? Are there significant sex differences? Significant status differences? Explain.

3.  What does the position you selected communicate to the person already seated? In what ways might this nonverbal message be misinterpreted? How would your subsequent nonverbal (and perhaps verbal) behavior reinforce your intended message? That is, what would you do to ensure that the message you intended to communicate is in fact the message communicated and received?

## 5.5 Theories About Space

"Protection theory" claims that the space around oneself serves as a body-buffer zone and serves a protective function. When one is being threatened, one's body-buffer zone expands; when we feel secure and safe, our body-buffer zone shrinks. For example, if we find ourselves in a strange and dangerous neighborhood and feel threatened, our body-buffer zone would probably expand and we would tend to avoid getting too close to those we might perceive as threatening. On the other hand, if we are with a group of close friends and feel secure, our body-buffer zone would shrink considerably and we would welcome close distances and mutual touching. [For more on protection theory see M. Dosey and M. Meisels, "Personal Space and Self-Protection," *Journal of Personality and Social Psychology*, 38 (1976):959-965.]

"Equilibrium theory," on the other hand, claims that intimacy and distance vary together; the higher the intimacy, the closer the distance; the lower the intimacy, the greater the distance. This theory claims, then, that we maintain close distances with those with whom we have close interpersonal relationships and that we maintain greater distances with those with whom we do not have close relationships. [For more on equilibrium theory see M. Argyle and J. Dean, "Eye Contact, Distance and Affiliation," *Sociometry* 28 (1965):289-304.]

Directions: In groups of five or six design and conduct a brief observational study to test one of the theories. Following these basic steps will make the exercise easier and more meaningful.

1. Develop a hypothesis.
   For this exercise, use a null hypothesis, a hypothesis that states there is no difference, for example: *There is no difference in the distance maintained by intimately involved couples and newly introduced couples.*

2. Define all relevant variables.
   For example, in this hypothesis you would need to define: distance, intimately involved couples, and newly introduced couples.

3. Identify the kinds of observations you will need to make. For example:
   a. Who will make the observations?
   b. Will these observations be verified? By whom?
   c. How will results of the observations be recorded?
   d. How many people will be observed?
   e. Will sex, age, race, educational level, or other variables be controlled? How?

4. What kind of results do you feel you would need to feel your theory is supported? Unsupported? [If you know statistics and research design, then you may set your level of statistical significance here. Otherwise, simply consider how many of your observations would have to be in the same direction for you to consider the theory supported or unsupported.

5. Conduct your observations.

6. Summarize your findings so that they can easily be understood by others.

7. Formulate your conclusions and relate these back to your hypothesis. Generally, we seek to reject the null hypothesis. We seek to find a difference and thus reject the assumption or hypothesis that there is no difference. Can you reject the null hypothesis? We generally do not accept the null hypothesis even if we find no differences. The reason for this seemingly strange practice is simply that we assume that there are differences in the world; when we do not find them we cannot conclude that they do not exist, only that we have not—in this present study—found the differences.

8. Explain what you have learned from this exercise in designing and conducting an observational study in nonverbal communication.

9. On the basis of your study, what new and/or improved studies would you suggest be undertaken?

# 5.6 Observational Record of Spatial Communication

This observational record form is designed to increase your awareness of the forms and functions of spatial communication and its role in the total communication act. For each example of spatial communication noted, (1) describe the specific manifestation of that communication, and indicate (2) the sources and receivers of the message; (3) the specific context in which the communication occurred; (4) the message or meanings that were communicated; (5) the effects of the nonverbal communication; and (6) any additional comments or questions that you feel are relevant to understanding the specific communication.

Territoriality:

Marker (central, boundary, and ear):

Territorial encroachment:

Reactions to territorial encroachment:

Intimate distance:

Personal distance:

Social distance:

Public distance:

# Review and Discussion Questions

1. Explain the ways in which the various different distances communicate? How do you communicate differently when in these various distances?

2. Examine your own living space. How effectively is it arranged for the type of communication that usually takes place in that space? Comment on both the positive and the negative features.How might it be improved?

3. Under what conditions do you feel "crowded"? What satisfies your need for privacy? That is, in what kind of environment do you experience the feelings of privacy?

4. How is territoriality evidenced in your own living space? What happens when a territory is invaded? Who "owns" the largest territory? Who "owns" the least territory? How does this territorial pattern reflect or refute our traditional sex roles?

5. Is territoriality evidenced in your classroom? In what ways? How is territorial invasion responded to?

6. In the discussion of territorial encroachment, three major types were singled out: violation, invasion, and contamination. Provide at least one example from your own experience, from literature, from the media, or from history of each of these forms of territorial encroachment.

7. We can react to territorial encroachment in a number of ways. The four ways that were identified were: (a) turf defense, insulation, linguistic collusion, and withdrawal. Provide at least one example from your own experience, from literature, from the media, or from history of each of these forms of reactions to territorial encroachment.

8. One of the ways in which we indicate our ownership of a territory is to mark it. Provide at least one additional example for each of the three types of markers identified in this chapter: central, boundary, and ear markers.

# Terms to Define

Proxemics

Proxemic distances

Intimate distance

Personal distance

Social distance

Public distance

Proxemic influences

Territoriality

Crowding

Density

Privacy

Surveillance

Behavioral constraint

Stimulus overload

Territorial encroachment

Violation

Invasion

Contamination

Withdrawal

Turf defense

Insulation

Linguistic collusion

Primary territory

Secondary territory

Public territory

Markers

Central marker

Boundary marker

Ear marker

Protection theory

Equilibrium theory

Additional relevant terms in spatial communication

# 6
# Tactile Communication

## Chapter Outline

The Functions of Touch
Differences in Touch Communication
*Gender Differences*
*Status Differences*
*Cultural Differences*
*Other Variables*
Touch Avoidance

Tactile Communication Exercises

6.1 Body Accessibility
6.2 Touch Avoidance
6.3 The Varied Embrace
6.4 Rules of Tactile Communication
6.5 The Communicative Handshake
6.6 Observational Record of Touch
     Communication

Review and Discussion Questions
Terms to Define

## Objectives

After completing this chapter, you should be able to:

1. define *haptics*
2. provide examples for each of the five major functions of touch: functional-professional, social-polite, friendship-warmth, love-intimacy, and sexual arousal
3. provide examples of gender, status, and cultural differences in touch communication
4. explain the nature of *touch avoidance* and some of the variables which influence it

Tactile communication is probably the first form of communication we experience. As infants we learn about the world around us largely by touching. We learn about our own bodies through touching. Throughout our infant and then our adult life we touch and are touched for a wide variety of purposes.

# The Functions of Touch

One of the most popular classifications of touching functions identifies five major functions: functional-professional, social polite, friendship-warmth, love-intimacy, and sexual arousal.

Mothers and fathers may prepare food for us, they may chauffeur us around, they may give us money to buy an ice-cream cone or go to a movie, but nothing they do registers as deeply on us as do their squeezes, pats, strokes and embraces. It is not what our families give to us or do for us that makes us feel their love, it is our bodily sensations when they touch us. Tactile sensations become our emotions. We can receive no greater assurance of our worth and our lovability than to be affectionately touched and held in the cradle of family life. Knowing that we are valued sends us into the world with some magical inner strength to deflect life's slings and arrows.

Helen Colton, *Touch Therapy* (New York: Kensington Publishing, 1983), p. 58.

**Functional-Professional.** In functional-professional touching the touch does something for the person as when, for example, the dentist manipulates our mouth or the hairdresser moves our head.

**Social-Polite.** Social-polite touching functions to create a connection between two people as, for example, when we shake hands or kiss someone on the cheek.

**Friendship-Warmth.** When we touch for the purpose of friendship-warmth we tell the other person, through our touch, that we like him or her. That is, our touch communicates a positive feeling for the other person.

**Love and Intimacy.** Love and intimacy are communicated largely through hugging and kissing.

**Sexual Arousal.** Sexual arousal is likewise communicated through hugging and kissing but also through fondling, petting, and sexual intercourse.

---

Touch may be viewed as negative when it is used unilaterally. When one person has access to another person's body, but the first person is not allowed the same privilege in return, touch becomes an indicator of status rather than of solidarity. In this light, touch may be viewed as the ultimate invasion of personal space. When we consider the variety of contexts in which unilateral touching occurs, e.g., doctors touching nurses, customers touching waitresses, teachers touching students, managers touching subordinates, police officers touching accused persons, counselors touching clients, and ministers touching parishioners, it becomes evident that touch demonstrates power or status in these contexts. . . . We can determine whether touch is reciprocal or unilateral by considering whether the superior would view initiation of touch by the subordinate as appropriate. For instance, may the waitress initiate touch with the customer, may the student touch the teacher's arm, may the accused touch the police officer in the same manner as he or she has been touched, and so nurses have the same access to physicians' bodies as they sometimes appear to have to the nurses?

Judy Cornelia Pearson, *Gender and Communication*
(Dubuque, Iowa: Brown, 1985), p. 255.

---

# Differences in Touch Communication

If we examine the ways we touch and the functions that touch serves, we find a number of significant differences.

## Gender Differences

One of the most striking differences to observe is frequency of touch for men and women. Men and women do not touch with the same frequency or in the same way nor are they touched with the same frequency or in the same way. For example, women are touched more than men; girl babies are touched more than boy babies. Similarly, mothers touch their children a great deal more than do fathers. Some of these differences are explored in the exercises in this chapter.

## Status Differences

Another important variable that influences touch is status. Generally, it is found that higher status people will initiate touch with lower status people rather than the reverse. For example, doctors will touch nurses more than nurses will touch doctors. Managers will touch workers more than workers will touch management.

Within social classes, however, high status people generally touch a great deal less than do lower status people. High level white-collar workers, for example, will engage in significantly less mutual touching than will blue-collar workers.

> "There is a very simple rule about touching," the manager continued. "*When you touch, don't take.* Touch the people you manage only when you are *giving* them something—reassurance, support, encouragement, whatever."
>
> "So you should refrain from touching someone," the young man said, "until you know them and they know you are interested in their success—that you are clearly on their side. I can see that."
>
> Kenneth Blanchard and Spencer Johnson, *The One Minute Manager* (New York: Berkley Books, 1982), p. 95.

## Cultural Differences

Cultures differ widely in their touch norms. Some cultures encourage touching among all its members regardless of gender. Other cultures discourage touching among all its members. Most cultures encourage certain types of touching and discourage others. For example, in Japan there are strong touch avoidance norms, especially against strangers. In their interactions the Japanese are especially careful to maintain proper distance so that touching will not take place. Mediterranean and Latin American people, on the other hand, will engage in a great deal of touching. Men, for example, will often walk with their arms around each other's shoulders. In the United States there are norms that encourage men to initiate opposite-sex touching and for superiors to initiate touch with subordinates.

## Other Variables

Other variables influencing touching behavior are the age, race, relational status, the degree of comfort felt, the attitudes we wish to communicate, and the feelings we have for the other person.

# Touch Avoidance

Much as we communicate by touching, we also communicate by not touching or by touch avoidance. We each have a desire to touch—for some this is a particularly strong desire, even a need; for others, the desire is relatively weak. Similarly, we each have a tendency to avoid touching others and being touched by others.

> If those humans closest to us cannot supply us with what we want, and if it is too dangerous to seek intimacies with strangers, then we can make tracks to the nearest pet shop and, for a small sum, buy ourselves a piece of animal intimacy. For pets are innocent; they cause no problems and they ask no questions. They lick our hands, they rub softly up against our legs, they curl up to sleep on our thighs, and they nuzzle us. We can cuddle them, stroke them, pat them, carry them like babies, tickle them behind the ears, and even kiss them.
>
> Desmond Morris, *Intimate Behaviour* (New York: Bantam, 1971), pp. 184-185.

It has been found, for example, that although men have low touch avoidance scores for opposite-sex touching, they have high touch avoidance scores for same-sex touching. Women, on the other hand, have high touch avoidance scores for opposite-sex touching but low touch avoidance scores for same-sex touching. This gender difference probably reflects the different conditioning history of men and women and the societal rules and norms that encourage men in opposite-sex touching and women in same-sex touching and discourage men in same-sex touching and women in opposite-sex touching.

It has also been found that persons who are fearful of communication—those who have great communication apprehension— will also tend to avoid communication by touch. Similarly, those who are low self-disclosers also avoid touch communication. Self-disclosure and touching are both intimate forms of interpersonal interaction and so it is natural that if a person avoid one form of this intimate interaction, he or she will also avoid the other form.

Older persons generally avoid opposite-sex touching more than do younger people. However, the older and the younger seem to engage in approximately equal same-sex touching.

A scale to measure touch avoidance, developed by Peter Andersen and Ken Leibowitz, on whose research this discussion was based, is included in the exercises.

---

Our bodies, our nervous system, our satisfactions with other people, and our creativity might be greatly enhanced if we simply touch more. Hands particularly can carry life-giving energy when these hands have learned how to be sensitive. Hands aren't only for work, punishment, and sex. They are very much a very believable human means of making contact.

Virginia Satir, *Making Contact* (Berkeley, Calif.: Celestial Arts, 1976).

---

# Tactile Communication Exercises

The tactile communication exercises provided here aim to raise your consciousness of the ways in which touch communicates: what we communicate when we touch and what others communicate when they touch us. In *Body Accessibility* we examine the touching we receive from our mothers, fathers, same-sex friend, and opposite-sex friend and then compare these with the results of other studies to see if there are significant differences and to speculate on the reasons for these differences. The *Touch Avoidance* test enable us to estimate our own tendency to avoid same-sex and opposite-sex touching and to then compare our scores with those derived from previous studies. Some of the variables influencing touch avoidance are also noted here.

In *The Varied Embrace* we explore twelve different ways in which we can embrace another person and consider such factors as the meanings these embraces communicate, the context in which they are likely to occur, the gender of the person who would normally initiate the embrace, and the probable relational status of the people involved. In *Rules of Tactile Communication* we examine the rules operating in our culture for touch communication and explore how these rules would differ on the basis of the gender of the people involved and their relationship to each other.

In *The Communicative Handshake* we dissect the everyday handshake and seek to consider the varied messages that this ''simple'' touch can communicate. This exercise is also designed to heighten your awareness of the messages that your own handshake communicates. The *Observational Record of Touch Communication* is designed to increase your awareness of your touching behavior, its forms and functions, and its role in the whole communication act.

# 6.1 Body Accessibility

Assume that the figures below are of your body.

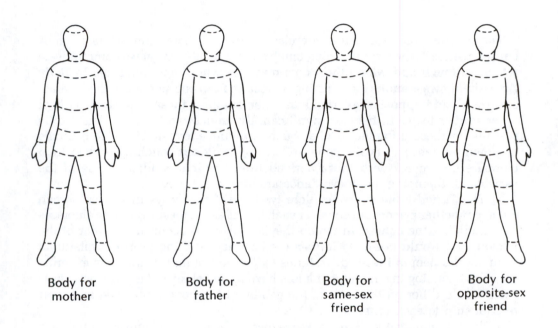

Body for
mother

Body for
father

Body for
same-sex
friend

Body for
opposite-sex
friend

1. The first figure is your body as touched by your mother.
2. The second figure is your body as touched by your father.
3. The third figure is your body as touched by your closest friend of the same sex.
4. The fourth figure is your body as touched by your closest friend of the opposite sex.

Indicate the frequency with which each part of your body is or has been touched by the four persons named. Use the following scale:

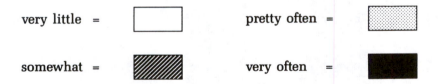

After you have completed these figures, form groups of five or six and discuss your findings. It may prove useful to organize your discussion around such questions as the following:

1. Do your mothers touch you more than your fathers?

2. Does the amount of touching and the location of the touching depend on your sex?

3. Where (e.i., what body parts) do mothers touch most?

4. Where do fathers touch most?

5. Do same sex or opposite sex friends touch you more?

6. Do same sex or opposite sex friends touch you in the same places?

7. Does the amount and location of touching by same sex friends depend on whether you are male or female?

8. Does the amount and location of touching by opposite sex friends depend on whether you are male or female?

9. By whom is a male touched most?

10. By whom is a female touched most?

11. Are these patterns of touch the same in different cultures?

12. Are these patterns of touch stable over time or do they change over time, say, from one generation to the next?

After you have discussed these figures, examine those on the following page. How do your figures compare to those obtained from these other studies? How might you account for the differences?

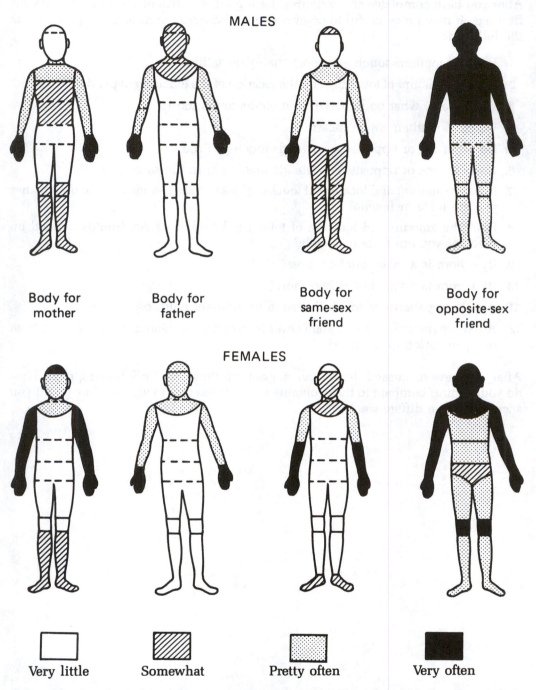

The amount of touching of the various parts of the body as reported by male and female college students.
*Source:* From S. M. Jourard, "An Exploratory Study of Body-Accessibility," *British Journal of Social and Clinical Psychology* 5(1966):221-231.

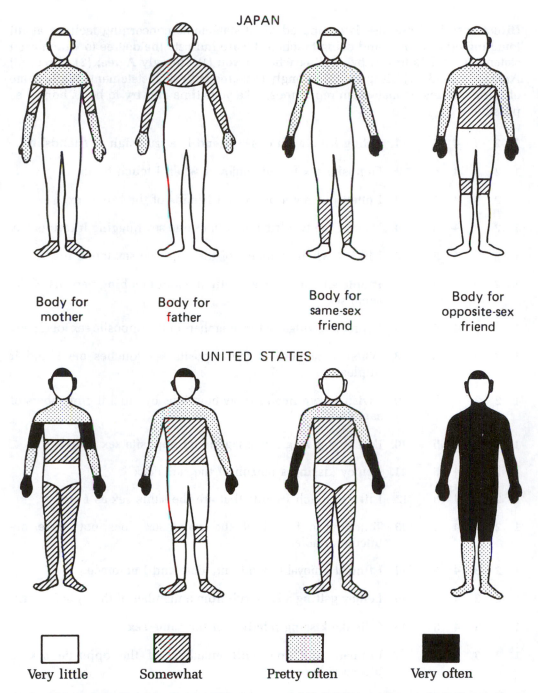

Areas and frequency of touching as reported by Japanese and United States college students. *Source:* From Dean C. Barnlund, "Communicative Styles in Two Cultures: Japan and the United States," in A. Kendon, R. M. Harris, and Mr. R. Key, eds., *Organization of Behavior in Face-to-Face Interaction* (The Hague: Mouton, 1975).

# 6.2 Touch Avoidance*

**Directions:** This exercise is composed of 18 statements concerning feelings about touching other people and being touched. Please indicate the degree to which each statement applies to you by circling whether you (1) Strongly Agree; (2) Agree; (3) Are Undecided; (4) Disagree; (5) Strongly Disagree with each statement. While some of these statements may seem repetitious, take your time and try to be as honest as possible.

1  2  3  4  5    1. A hug from a same sex friend is a true sign of friendship.

1  2  3  4  5    2. Opposite sex friends enjoy it when I touch them.

1  2  3  4  5    3. I often put my arm around friends of the same sex.

1  2  3  4  5    4. When I see two friends of the same sex hugging it revolts me.

1  2  3  4  5    5. I like it when members of the opposite sex touch me.

1  2  3  4  5    6. People shouldn't be so uptight about touching persons of the same sex.

1  2  3  4  5    7. I think it is vulgar when members of the opposite sex touch me.

1  2  3  4  5    8. When a member of the opposite sex touches me I find it unpleasant.

1  2  3  4  5    9. I wish I were free to show emotions by touching members of same sex.

1  2  3  4  5    10. I'd enjoy giving a massage to an opposite sex friend.

1  2  3  4  5    11. I enjoy kissing a person of the same sex.

1  2  3  4  5    12. I like to touch friends that are the same sex as I am.

1  2  3  4  5    13. Touching a friend of the same sex does not make me uncomfortable.

1  2  3  4  5    14. I find it enjoyable when my date and I embrace.

1  2  3  4  5    15. I enjoy getting a back rub from a member of the opposite sex.

1  2  3  4  5    16. I dislike kissing relatives of the same sex.

1  2  3  4  5    17. Intimate touching with members of the opposite sex is pleasurable.

1  2  3  4  5    18. I find it difficult to be touched by a member of my own sex.

In order to score your Touch Avoidance Questionnaire, follow these procedures:

1. Reverse your scores for items 4, 7, 8, 16, and 18. Use these reversed scores in all future calculations.

2. To obtain your same-sex touch avoidance score (the extent to which you avoid touching members of your own sex): total the scores for items 1, 3, 4, 6, 9, 11, 12, 13, 16, and 18.

3. To obtain your opposite-sex touch avoidance score (the extent to which you avoid touching members of the opposite sex): total the scores for items 2, 5, 7, 8, 10, 14, 15, and 17.

4. To obtain your total touch avoidance score, add the subtotals from steps 2 and 3.

   The higher the score, the higher the touch avoidance, that is, the greater your tendency to avoid touch.

Among the findings pertaining to touch avoidance are these:

1. Touch avoidance is positively related to communication apprehension. The more apprehensive a person is concerning communication, the more he or she will avoid touching.

2. Touch avoidance is negatively related to self disclosure. Low self-disclosives will have high touch avoidance scores. People who disclose little will also touch little; people who disclose a great deal will also touch a great deal.

3. Men evidence greater same-sex touch avoidance while women evidence greater opposite-sex touch avoidance.

4. Older marrieds evidence higher levels of opposite-sex touch avoidance whereas no opposite-sex touch avoidance differences were found for young marrieds.

What relationships would you predict might exist between touch avoidance the following variables:

1. Race: Do different races have different touch avoidance tendencies? Explain.

2. Empathy: Do persons of high and low empathy have different touch avoidance tendencies? Explain.

3. Educational level: Do educated and uneducated persons differ in their touch avoidance tendencies? Explain.

4. Urban v. rural life-style: Do touch avoidance tendencies vary on the basis of whether one lives in an urban or a rural environment? Explain.

What other factors do you think might influence one's tendency toward touch avoidance?

*From Peter A. Andersen and K. Leibowitz, "The Development and Nature of Touch Avoidance," *Environmental Psychology and Nonverbal Behavior* (1978):89-106. Reprinted by permission of Peter Andersen.

# 6.3 The Varied Embrace

For each of the dozen types of embraces noted here, identify:

**Meanings:** the primary meaning communicated by this gesture

**Contexts:** appropriate and likely or inappropriate and unlikely contexts for this type of embrace

**Gender:** the probable sex of the "initiator" and of the "receiver" of the embrace

**Relational status:** the most probable and the least probable relational status of the two parties

1. The full embrace

2. The shoulder embrace

3. The hand-on-shoulder embrace

4. The arm-link embrace

5. The hand-in-hand embrace

6. The hand-head contact embrace

7. The head-head contact embrace

8. The kissing embrace (lips, cheek, top of head, hurt finger, things [dice, rabbit's foot, religious article], other's hand, one's own hand)

9. The handshake embrace

10. The hand to waist embrace

11. The hand-around-torso embrace

12. The hand-on-hip/hand-on-buttocks embrace

This exercise is based on Desmond Morris's [*Intimate Behavior* (New York: Random House, 1971)] discussion of social intimacy.

# 6.4   Rules of Tactile Communication

Identify three rules operating in our culture for *tactile communication* in an inter-personal interaction between two men who are close friends. [Note: rules may be conceived of as prescriptive (indicating what should be done) or as proscriptive (indicating what should not be done).]

1.



2.



3.



Identify three rules operating in our culture for *tactile communication* in an inter-personal interaction between two women who are close friends. Note specifically how these rules differ from those identified above.

1.



2.



3.

Identify three rules operating in our culture for *tactile communication* in an interpersonal interaction between a woman and a man who are close friends. Note specifically how these rules differ from those identified above.

1.

2.

3.

Review the nine rules you have identified and respond to the following:

1.  What do these rules communicate? That is, what messages do these rules send out to the participants as well as to outside observers?

2.  Are these rules cross-cultural or culture-specific? If possible, give examples of these same rules or contradictory rules operating in other cultures.

3.  Do you think these rules are changing? In what direction are they changing? Why are(n't) they changing?

# 6.5  The Communicative Handshake

The purpose of this brief exercise is to identify some of the meanings communicated by the handshake and some of the nonverbal behaviors that accompany different types of handshakes and to heighten awareness of the messages our own handshakes may communicate to others.

Groups of four persons are formed.

*Before reading any further,* all four members should shake hands so that each member shakes hands with each other member at least once.

Two members are designated observers and two performers (A and B). A will serve as the principal subject or "actor" while B serves as the "recipient" of the handshake message. The two observers should watch the interaction carefully and then record their observations on the form provided.

The procedures are as follows: Performer A should read the list of feeling states provided below and shake hands with Performer B while role playing each of these feeling states. Performer B should mentally note how he or she felt about each handshake.

After all five feeling states have been portrayed, Performer B becomes the "actor" and Performer A becomes the "recipient." The procedure is then repeated. Next, the observers become performers and the procedure is again repeated until each person has served as actor, recipient, and observer.

After all interactions have been completed, the observers' forms should be analyzed and the feedback from the recipients should be discussed.

*Feeling States*

1. I'm feeling nervous and uncomfortable in this setting.

2. I'm totally in control of myself and of the situation; I feel confident and perfectly at ease.

3. I feel down, depressed; I have a low self-concept and generally think of myself as inadequate.

4. I like you and I want you to like me.

5. I want you to think of me as friendly, outgoing, and an all around good person.

## Observation Form

**Instructions:** Observers should pay special attention to the following four areas of nonverbal behavior and should record what they observe during these several handshakes. Observers may confer with each other (but should not let the performers hear) and complete one form jointly or they may complete their forms independently and then confer with each other and compile a composite form. These forms will then be given to the performers and discussed with them after the entire exercise is completed.

---

1. *I'm feeling nervous and uncomfortable:*

Facial expressions:

Eye movements and contact:

Body posture and orientation:

Physical closeness and touching:

---

2. *I'm totally in control; I feel confident:*

Facial expressions:

Eye movements and contact:

Body posture and orientation:

Physical closeness and touching:

---

3. *I feel down; depressed:*

Facial expressions:

Eye movements and contact:

Body posture and orientation:

Physical closeness and touching:

4. *I like you and I want you to like me:*

Facial expressions:

Eye movements and contact:

Body posture and orientation:

Physical closeness and touching:

5. *I want you to think of me as friendly, outgoing:*

Facial expressions:

Eye movements and contact:

Body posture and orientation:

Physical closeness and touching:

# 6.6   Observational Record of Touch Communication

This observational record form is designed to increase your awareness of the forms and functions of touch communication and its role in the total communication act. For each example of touch communication noted, (1) describe the specific manifestation of that communication, and indicate (2) the sources and receivers of the message; (3) the specific context in which the communication occurred; (4) the message or meanings that were communicated; (5) the effects of the nonverbal communication; and (6) any additional comments or questions that you feel are relevant to understanding the specific communication.

Functional-professional touch:


Social-polite touch:


Friendship-warmth touch:


Love-intimacy touch:


Sexual arousal touch:


Touch avoidance:


Body contact tie sign:


Handshake:


Self-intimacy behaviors:

# Review and Discussion Questions

1. Was your own touch experience (as evidenced in the "body accessibility" exercise) consistent with the results found by previous researchers? In what ways was it consistent? In what ways was it inconsistent? How do you account for these consistencies and inconsistencies?

2. How did your own score on "Touch Avoidance" compare to those derived from previous research? If there are significant differences, how do you account for these?

3. Each person has various body contact needs, the need to touch and to be touched. In what situations are your body contact needs greatest? Least? Why?

4. What messages did your family communicate to you regarding the appropriateness and inappropriateness of touch? That is, can you identify the rules for touching and being touched that you were taught when you were growing up?

5. Among the meanings that touch communicates are: positive affect, playfulness, control, ritualistic functions, and task related functions. Provide at least one example of how touch can communicate each of these five meanings.

6. How does touch figure into impression formation? That is, how do you form impressions of people on the basis of the way in which they touch others as well as they way in which they respond to the touch of others?

# Terms to Define

Tactile communication

Haptics

Functional-professional touching

Social-polite touching

Friendship-warmth touching

Love-intimacy touching

Sexual arousal touching

Touch avoidance

Touch norms

Additional relevant terms in tactile communication

# 7

# Paralanguage and Silence

## Chapter Outline

Paralanguage
Paralanguage Dimensions
    *Voice Qualities*
    *Vocalizations*
People Judgments
Effectiveness Judgments
Conversational Turns
    *Turn-maintaining*
    *Turn-yielding*
    *Turn-requesting*
    *Turn-denying*
    *Back-channeling*
Silence
    *Cultural Differences*

Paralanguage and Silence Exercises

7.1 Statements: Positive and Negative
7.2 Paralinguistically Speaking
7.3 Paralanguage Communication
7.4 Communicating Emotions
    Paralinguistically
7.5 Conversational Turns
7.6 The Functions of Silence
7.7 Observational Record of Para-
    language and Silence
    Communication

Review and Discussion Questions
Terms to Define

## Objectives

After completing this chapter, you should be able to:

1. define *paralanguage* and its two major dimensions: voice qualities and vocalizations
2. explain the role of paralanguage in making judgments about people and in judging effectiveness
3. explain the concept of conversational turns and define each of the five basic types: turn-maintaining, turn-yielding, turn-requesting, turn-denying, and back-channeling
4. define *silence*

In this unit we consider paralanguage and silence. While these two dimensions of nonverbal often escape our attention, they are extremely important in communication and convey a wide variety of messages.

# Paralanguage

*Paralanguage* refers to the vocal but nonverbal dimension of communication. Paralanguage refers to the manner in which something is said rather than to what is said. Included in paralanguage are a wide variety of vocal features, for example, rate, volume, pitch, pausing and hesitations, and rhythm.

[Paralanguage is] the study of all cues in oral speech other than the content of the words spoken.

Malandro and Barker, p. 25

# Paralanguage Dimensions

Paralanguage may be defined as the vocal but nonverbal dimension of speech. Paralanguage consists of those audible elements that accompany the words we speak. There are two major areas of paralanguage: voice qualities and vocalizations.

## Voice Qualities

This category includes those qualities of speech that can be separated (for purposes of analysis, at least) from the specific sounds and words that are spoken. Voice qualities consist of such elements as pitch (the highness or lowness of tone), rhythm (for example, whether smooth or jerky), resonance (ranging from resonant to thin), and rate (the number of words spoken per unit of time).

## Vocalizations

This category includes vocal characterizers (for example, laughing and crying, yelling and whispering), vocal qualifiers (for example, intensity or volume which can range from overly loud to overly soft and "extent" which can range from the stereotypical Southern drawl to the clipped speaking style of a harried executive), and vocal segregates (for example, uh-uh, sh, and the pause).

---

The field of paralinguistics has developed in two major directions: voice as indicator of personality and voice as indicator of the state of the interaction. Both areas depend on the voice as a conveyor of emotion. Prominent in the first tradition have been the voice and personality studies, which have generally shown that raters have stereotyped conceptions of which vocal qualities indicate which personality traits. . . . Logically prior to the step of equating personality type and speech is the smaller step of establishing the link between emotion and voice.

Weitz, p. 224

---

# People Judgments

On the basis of paralinguistic cues, we formulate numerous impressions of others. For example, research shows that we can correctly identify the sex, status, and approximate age of the speaker solely from paralanguage cues. Further, we can also judge the emotional state of a speaker from paralanguage cues. Of course, some emotions are easier to communicate paralinguistically than are others. For example, anger seems easier to communicate and to recognize than fear or jealousy.

# Effectiveness Judgments

Variations in paralinguistic qualities can greatly influence the ways in which messages are perceived. In a study of speaking rate (the normal speaking rate being 140 words per minute) people agreed most with the speaker who spoke rapidly (at 191 words per minute) and least with the speaker who spoke less rapidly (111 words per minute).

In terms of comprehension, 141 words per minute was determined to be 100 percent understood. When the rate was increased to 201 words per minute, the comprehension rate was only reduced to 95 percent. When the rate was further increased to 282 words per minute, (double the normal rate) the comprehension rate was still a reasonably high 90 percent.

We tend to believe the speaker who speaks at a somewhat faster rate more than we do the speaker who speaks at a normal or slower-than-normal rate—unless we have reason to suspect the speaker has something to gain or is trying to put one over on us. If you listen carefully to television endorsements, you will find that the speakers generally speak at a faster-than-normal rate. Not only does this enable them to get more of their message communicated but it also, apparently, helps in their attempt to persuade their audience. Interestingly enough, listeners also seem to prefer a rate somewhat faster than normal.

# Conversational Turns

We also make judgments about conversational turns, the exchanging of speaker and listener roles in a conversation. We may distinguish five major conversational turns.

## Turn-maintaining Cues

In turn-maintaining the speaker wishes to maintain the role of speaker and signals to others that he or she is not finished yet. Vocalized pauses (er, em, and the like) are perhaps the most obvious way to indicate that one is not finished speaking.

## Turn-yielding Cues

Turn-yielding cues are used when the speaker wishes that someone else take the role of speaker. A rising intonation, as in asking a question, or a falling intonation that indicates completion of a thought are among the most common paralanguage turn-yielding cues. The clearest and most obvious turn-yielding cue, of course, is simply to ask the listener a question.

## Turn-requesting Cues

Through turn-requesting cues the listener indicates his or her wish to speak. When a listener vocalizes an *er* or *ah*, for example, it usually signals a desire to take a turn as speaker.

## Turn-denying Cues

In turn-denying the speaker passes the turn to the listener but the listener denies the turn as speaker indicating that the listener does not wish to speak at this time. Students will often engage in turn-denying by avoiding eye-contact with the teacher, especially after a specific question has been asked and the teacher visually searches the room for someone to call on. We could also signal this paralinguistically by pretending to cough or blow one's nose or by mumbling sounds that resemble "don't know."

## Back-channeling Cues

In back-channeling, the listener indicates the desire for the speaker to continue in the role of speaker. Giving the speaker positive, reinforcing cues (for example, *hmm*) are perhaps the best way to back-channel.

---

**Speech is civilization itself. The word, even the most contradictory word, preserves contact; it is silence which isolates.**

**Thomas Mann**

---

# Silence

*Silence*, of course, is the absence of speech. but it is not the absence of communication. Through silence we serve a variety of communication functions. For example, silence allows the speaker time to think. We can hurt someone by giving them "the silent treatment." This technique is a particularly damaging conflict strategy because it prevents us from talking about the very matters that are now causing difficulties. In *The Functions of Silence* exercise, eleven such functions are identified.

We may also use silence to isolate ourselves and to prevent further communication. We use silence to communicate emotional responses; for example, defiance of authority or determination to be uncooperative may be effectively signalled by silence.

---

**Silence is nothing merely negative; it is not the mere absence of speech. It is a positive, a complete world in itself.**

**Max Picard**

---

## Cultural Differences

As with most of nonverbal communication, there are large cultural differences in the use of silence from one culture to another. For example, in the United States girls and boys on dates are expected to talk a great deal. The objective of the dating experience is for the young people to get to know each other. Among the Apache, however, women who talk a great deal with their dates are thought to betray prior experience with men. At times, it is seen as indicating the woman's willingness to engage in sexual relations.

Similarly, in the United States newly introduced persons are expected to engage in communication freely. Among the Apache, however, newly introduced persons would remain silent for long periods (several days is not uncommon) in order to give each person an opportunity to look over the other person.

# Paralanguage and Silence Exercises

The *Workbook* exercises are designed to illustrate the wide variety of communication functions that the seemingly insignificant dimensions of paralanguage and silence may serve. In *Statements: Positive or Negative* we explore how the same verbal statement may be said with a positive meaning and then with a negative meaning by varying paralinguistic cues. In *Paralinguistically Speaking* the same general procedure is used but this time the information you are asked to communicate is a bit more complex. Here you are asked to say the same sentence in order to communicate drastically different meanings through only paralanguage differences.

Both *Paralanguage Communication* and *Communicating Emotions Paralinguistically* illustrate the research technique of content free speech and how a variety of different emotions may be communicated paralinguistically. In *Conversational Turns* we focus on the five major turn-taking systems and how these are communicated paralinguistically. This exercise should serve to bring to consciousness the subtle cues that are used to communicate conversational turns and be useful to both speakers and listeners in communicating and in responding to these turn signals.

*The Functions of Silence* focuses on 11 functions of silence and asks that you supply a specific example illustrating each of these functions. *Observational Record of Paralanguage and Silence Communication* is designed to heighten your awareness of the forms and functions of paralanguage and silence and their role in the communication interaction.

# 7.1  Statements: Positive or Negative

The objective of this exercise is to demonstrate that the same verbal statement can communicate a positive or a negative meaning depending on the paralinguistic cues that accompany the statement. Each of the fifteen statements presented below should be read first to communicate a positive feeling or meaning and second to communicate a negative feeling or meaning. One procedure is to have the entire class seated in a circle and to go around the room with the first student reading statement No. 1 with a positive meaning, the second student reading statement No. 1 with a negative meaning, and so on until all 15 statements are read.

After all 15 statements are read with both the positive and negative perspectives, consider some or all of the following issues:

1. What paralinguistic cues communicate positive meaning? What paralinguistic cues communicate negative meaning?

2. What one paralinguistic cue was most helpful in enabling the speaker to communicate a positive or a negative meaning?

3. Most people would claim that it is easier to decode the positive or negative meanings than to encode these meanings. Was this true in this experience? Why do you suppose this is true?

4. Although this exercise focused on paralanguage, the statements were probably read with different facial expressions. What facial expressions were consistently used in the positive statements? What facial expressions were consistently used in the negative statements?

**Statements**

1. I really hate this.
2. I can't deal with this right now.
3. This isn't going to be easy but it's got to be done.
4. I can't begin to tell you what this means to me.
5. I sure won the prize this time, didn't I?
6. Wow! That was some date I had last night.
7. When will we be ready to try it?
8. Did I tell you what happened the other night?
9. Who could have expected that?
10. Is this true?
11. I refuse to believe that this happened.
12. It just doesn't make sense to me.
13. I really don't deserve this.
14. Do you know what happened to Pat and Chris last night?
15. I wish I could tell you how I really feel.

## 7.2 Paralinguistically Speaking

The objective of this exercise is to illustrate the varied meanings one can communicate through variation in paralinguistic features. Presented below are several sentences each of which may have a variety of specific meanings (indicated here by statements "a" through "e" or "f"). Indicate how you would speak each sentence to communicate each of the intended meanings.

1. *Tell me how Bobby proposed to you.*

   a. Hurry up, I'm dying to know.

   b. I know you don't tell others, but tell me.

   c. Bobby could really do a lot better than you.

   d. Bobby is a really shy person; how did he ever propose?

   e. I too was just proposed to; how were you proposed to?

2. *Is this the creep you want me to date?*

   a. Of all the creeps, is this the one you want me to date?

   b. You're being insulting to me by suggesting that I date this creep; I can easily do a lot better.

   c. I might talk with this creep but I would never go out on a date.

   d. This person is a real creep.

   e. I can't believe that my best friend wants me to date this creep.

3. *I had a night last night that you would never believe.*

   a. It was horrible.

   b. It was great.

   c. It was totally strange and unexpected.

   d. It was so great, I want you to tease it out of me.

   e. It was totally unbelievable.

   f. It was so totally inconsistent with what you know of me that you would never believe I did what I did.

4. *I love Pat and I love Chris.*

    a. Of course, I love Pat a lot more than Chris.

    b. Of course, I love Chris a lot more than Pat.

    c. I know I love Pat and I think I might love Chris too.

    d. I love Pat as a friend, but I love Chris as a lover.

    e. I don't love either.

5. *I really need this job at Robotics.*

    a. No one else needs this job like I do.

    b. It is not a question of wanting the job; I need it for survival.

    c. Of all the jobs I applied for, I need the one at Robotics.

    d. Of all the jobs at Robotics, I need this specific job.

    e. I'm fed up with this job at Robotics.

# 7.3 Paralanguage Communication*

In this exercise a subject recites the alphabet while attempting to communicate each of the following emotions:

| | |
|---|---|
| anger | nervousness |
| fear | pride |
| happiness | sadness |
| jealousy | satisfaction |
| love | sympathy |

The subject may begin the alphabet at any point and may omit and repeat sounds, but the subject may use only the names of the letters of the alphabet to communicate these feelings.

The subject should first number the emotions in random order so that he or she will have a set order to follow that is unknown to the audience, whose task it will be to guess the emotions expressed.

As a variation, have the subject go through the entire list of emotions: once facing the audience and employing any nonverbal signals desired and once with his or her back to the audience without employing any additional signals. Are there differences in the number of correct guesses depending on which method is used?

**For Discussion**

1. What are some of the differences between encoding and decoding "emotional meaning" and "logical meaning"?

2. Davitz and Davitz found the number of correct identifications for these emotions to be as follows: anger (156), nervousness (130), sadness (118), happiness (104), sympathy (93), satisfaction (75), love (60), fear (60), jealousy (69), and pride (50). Do these figures correspond to those you obtained? What conclusions would you draw about the relative ease or difficulty of expressing these emotions?

3. Do you think there is a positive relationship between encoding and decoding ability in situations such as this? Is the person who is adept at encoding the emotions also adept at decoding them? Explain.

4. What variables might influence encoding ability? Decoding ability?

5. What personality factors seem relevant to the encoding and decoding of emotions?

*This exercise is modeled on the research reported by Joel R. Davitz, *The Communication of Emotional Meaning* (New York: McGraw-Hill, 1964).

# 7.4   Communicating Emotions Paralinguistically

Read the sentences presented below while attempting to communicate the emotions indicated.* After you have practiced each of the sentences, indicate the paralinguistic cues you use to communicate the several emotions. For example, indicate pauses, words or syllables that are stressed, places where pitch changes would be introduced, words that are to be spoken with soft or loud volume, and so on.

Love:   There is no other answer. You've asked me that question a thousand times and my answer has always been the same; it will always be the same.

Happiness:   There is no other answer. You've asked me that question a thousand times and my answer has always been the same; it will always be the same.

Indifference:   There is no other answer. You've asked me that question a thousand times and my answer has always been the same; it will always be the same.

Sadness:   There is no other answer. You've asked me that question a thousand times and my answer has always been the same; it will always be the same.

Fear:   There is no other answer. You've asked me that question a thousand times and my answer has always been the same; it will always be the same.

Anger:   There is no other answer. You've asked me that question a thousand times and my answer has always been the same; it will always be the same.

In groups of five or six, speak these sentences and have group members attempt to guess the emotions you are trying to communicate. Each person should have a chance at communicating these six emotions. After each person has served as sender, respond to the following questions:

1. Are some emotions easier to communicate than others? For example, are negative emotions more accurately identified than are positive emotions?

2. Are males and females equally adept at communicating these emotions? At identifying these emotions? Is one sex superior at communicating or identifying some emotions while the other sex is superior at communicating or identifying other emotions?

3. What other variables might influence the ability to communicate and identify these emotions?

*These sentences were originally used by Grant Fairbanks, *Voice and Articulation Drillbook* (New York: Harper & Row, 1940). Robert C. Reardon used these sentences in his study on emotional expressions on which this exercise is based. See Reardon's, "Individual Differences and the Meanings of Vocal Emotional Expressions," *Journal of Communication* 21 (March 1971):72-82.

## 7.5 Conversational Turns

Much of our conversations are regulated through a process of exchanging the roles of speaker and listener. These exchanges are often signalled paralinguistically—through a wide range of vocalizations—as well as by various body gestures and facial and eye movements.

The purpose of this exercise is to explore these turn systems and to bring to consciousness the processes governing conversational turns.

The major conversational turns are these:

*Turn-maintaining:* the speaker wishes to maintain the role of speaker

*Turn-yielding:* the speaker announces to others in the conversation that the speaker has finished and it is now someone else's turn to speak

*Turn-requesting:* the listener wishes to speak, the listener wishes to assume the role of speaker

*Turn-denying:* the listener does not wish to assume the role of speaker

*Back-channeling:* the listener wants the speaker to continue in the role of speaker; the listener wishes to indicate a recognition of something the speaker says; (as a turn-denying cue) the listener indicates the unwillingness to exchange the role of listener for that of speaker

For each of these five conversational turns, indicate how each may be signalled paralinguistically *and* how it could be signalled through some other nonverbal means, for example, by body gestures, head movements, or facial and eye movements.

*Turn-maintaining*

Paralinguistic cues:

Other nonverbal cues:

*Turn-yielding*
Paralinguistic cues:

Other nonverbal cues:


*Turn-requesting*
Paralinguistic cues:

Other nonverbal cues:


*Turn-denying*
Paralinguistic cues:

Other nonverbal cues:


*Back-channeling:*
Paralinguistic cues:

Other nonverbal cues:



In addition, discussion may center around some or all of the following questions:

1.  What types of cues are especially effective in communciating one's conversational turn request?

2.  What types of cues are often ineffective? Why?

3.  What can one do when his or her conversational request is not responded to appropriately?

4.  Can you identify people of your acquaintance who are particularly insensitive or unresponsive to the conversational requests of others? How can you deal effectively with such people?

5.  How responsive are you to the conversational requests of others? How can you become more responsive and more sensitive?

## 7.6   The Functions of Silence

Researchers and observers of nonverbal communication have identified the following functions of silence. Explain in some depth how each of these functions may be served by silence and cite at least one example from a recent interpersonal interaction for each function.

Better to remain silent and be thought a fool than to speak out and remove all doubt.

Abraham Lincoln.

1. to provide thinking time

2. to hurt another person

3. to isolate oneself

4. to prevent communication

5. to communicate feelings

6. to create interpersonal distance

7. to signal respect and reverence

8. to provide a greater opportunity for increasing awareness of self and others

9. to accent or emphasize certain message units

10. to say "nothing"

11. to allow speaker to develop/explore own thoughts and feelings

## 7.7 Observational Record of Paralanguage and Silence Communication

This observational record form is designed to increase your awareness of the forms and functions of paralanguage and silence communication and their role in the total communication act. For each example of paralanguage and silence communication noted, (1) describe the specific manifestation of that communication, and indicate (2) the sources and receivers of the message; (3) the specific context in which the communication occurred; (4) the message or meanings that were communicated; (5) the effects of the nonverbal communication; and (6) any additional comments or questions that you feel are relevant to understanding the specific communication.

Volume variation:

Rate variation:

Pitch variation:

Pauses (filled and unfilled):

Nonstandard speech:

Turn yielding cue:

Turn requesting cue:

Turn denying cue:

Turn maintaining cue:

# Review and Discussion Questions

1. Define and explain the two major dimensions of paralanguage: voice qualities and vocalizations. Describe your own voice in terms of these dimensions? Ask others who know you well what they think of your voice. Are your descriptions similar? Different? Explain.

2. What do you suppose your voice communicates about you? For example, what does your voice communicate about your confidence? Assertiveness? Interest in the other person? Happiness or sadness? How can you go about testing your assumptions?

3. Examine the voices of several successful newscasters? What vocal features can you identify that contribute to their success? What do their voices have in common?

4. Do you make judgments of people on the basis of their voices? What types of judgments? How resistant are these judgments to later disconfirmation?

5. Describe the five major turn systems (maintaining, yielding, requesting, denying, and back-channeling) and vocally indicate how each of these may be communicated in an interactional situation.

6. Do you use silence as a weapon or as a conflict strategy? How do you use it? Is it effective in gaining the short term objective? Is it effective on a long term basis? That is, does the strategy do the relationship harm? Does it actually benefit the relationship?

7. Test your ability to decode emotions with these verbal descriptions. Are they descriptive of affection, anger, boredom, or joy?

   a. This voice is soft, with a low pitch, a resonant quality, a slow rate, and a steady and slightly upward inflection. The rhythm is regular, and the enunciation is slurred.

   b. This voice is loud, with a high pitch, a moderately blaring quality, a fast rate, an upward inflection, and a regular rhythm.

   c. This voice is loud, with a high pitch, a blaring quality, a fast rate, and an irregular up-and-down inflection. The rhythm is irregular, and the enunciation is clipped.

   d. This voice is moderate to low in volume, with a moderate-to-low pitch, a moderately resonant quality, a moderately slow rate, and a monotonous or gradually falling inflection. The enunciation is somewhat slurred.

On the basis of research conducted by Joel Davitz, the voices would communicate these emotions: a = affection; b = joy; c = anger; and d = boredom. How well did you do in identifying these emotions?

8. What cultural differences have you observed in the use of silence? What gender differences have you observed?

# Terms to Define

Paralanguage/paralinguistics

Conversational turn

Turn-maintaining cues

Turn-yielding cues

Turn-requesting cues

Turn-denying cues

Back-channeling cues

Voice qualities

Vocalizations

Silence

Additional relevant terms in paralanguage and silence communication

# 8
# Smell (Olfactics)

## Objectives

After completing this chapter, you should be able to:

1. define *olfactics*
2. explain the messages that smell is capable of communicating
3. provide examples of each of the olfactic phenomena considered here: smell blindness, smell adaptation, smell memory, smell overload, smell discrimination, and smell satiation
4. explain the relevance of smell differences to effective communication

Smell is one of those dimensions of nonverbal communication, an area we call *olfactics,* that is significant in a wide variety of situations. Yet, it is a dimension about which we know relatively little. We do know, for example, a great deal about the physiology of smell but we know little about its communicative dimension.

We do know that smell is important. Physiologically, we know that without smell, taste would be severely impaired. For example, it would be extremely difficult to taste the difference between a raw potato and an apple. Even tastes generally thought strong such as onion would have little taste without the accompanying smell.

Similarly, we know that in communication, smell influences a great deal. Advertisers and manufacturers are convinced of it and spend millions of dollars each year inserting nonfunctional scents into a variety of products we now identify by their smells such as cleaning products and toothpaste. More obviously, perfumes, colognes, after-shave lotions, deodorants, powders, and bath oils, for example, account for millions of dollars in sales daily. Our own behaviors of ritual bathing, usually with scented soap, wearing cologne (or some such variant), and using mouthwash and scented toothpaste attest to our own beliefs in the power of smell communication.

# Talking About Smells

Generally our vocabulary for talking about smell is rather limited and generally the terms that are available are rather vague. For example, consider the adjectives we have to describe smells: ambrosial, aromatic, fragrant, fetid, heady, musky, musty, pungent, putrid, rancid, rank, spicy, stinking, smelly, and scented. If you try to describe the smells denoted by each of these adjectives, you will probably have considerable difficulty.

> You can tell people they need a haircut or to wash their faces, but if you tell them they smell, you are really insulting.
>
> Winter, p. 16

Even dictionaries are of little help. For example, the *Random House Dictionary* defines rancid as "having a rank, unpleasant, stale smell," rank as "having an offensively strong smell," and stinking as "foul-smelling." Our own meanings, even with the aid of a good dictionary, identify the positive and negative quality of the adjective but do little beyond that to help us to define clearly a particular smell or to enable us to describe the way in which one smell differs from another.

In part, the difficulty in talking about smells is reflected by the lack of agreement among scientists in their identification and classification of smells. For example, in one classification popular at the turn of the century, six categories of primary smells were identified: fragrant, ethereal, resinous, spicy, putrid, empyreumatic (a burned smell). H. Zwaardemaker, in his 1925 *L'Odorat* used an eight part classification: aromatic, fragrant, ambrosial, alliaceous, hircine, repulsive, nauseous, ethereal, and empyreumatic. Today, physiologists say there may be as many as fifty primary smell sensations. Combinations of these primary odors can produce thousands of smell sensations.

# The Messages of Smell

Smell can communicate a wide variety of messages, many of which we seldom think about. Here are several common messages that smell communicates.

## Messages of Attraction

Perhaps the most obvious is that smell is used to send messages that will attract others to us. A great deal of animal communication serves this function. In many species, for example, females give off a particular odor that draws males, often from great distances, to these receptive females. In this way, the continuation of the species is assured

---

*Generally, Americans do not rely on their sense of smell for interpersonal cues unless perspiration odor, breath, or some other smell is unusually strong. Some believe that this olfactory repression reflects an antisensual American bias.*

*Knapp, pp. 169-170*

---

even though the males and females may be separated by long distances. Research is currently being conducted on using scents to stimulate and to suppress animal reproduction. That is, the scents not only arouse the individual animals and signal readiness, but they might also stimulate and suppress the physiological processes that contribute to reproduction.

Animals, of course, also use smell to repel invaders. Dogs, for example, will frequently urinate around what they consider their territory and will defend that territory against intruders such as strangers or other dogs. The urine warns other dogs that this is marked territory, owned by the scent-provider. Bees, for example, use scent to recognize members of their own colony. When a bee approaches the hive without the appropriate scent, it is forced away and frequently killed.

Humans, of course, use perfumes, colognes, after-shave lotions, powders, and the like to make ourselves smell more attractive to others. Sophia Loren, Elizabeth Taylor, and Dionne Warwick, to name just three, are selling perfumes by associating their own glamour and attractiveness with the fragrance of the perfume. The implication, of course, is that others can smell likewise and can appear equally attractive.

The obsession we have with eliminating our own body odor and with substituting the odor of some perfume creates an interesting if somewhat strange situation. Flora Davis, in her *Inside Intuition: What We Know About Nonverbal Communication*, observes: "One must admit that there's something more than a little bit ludicrous about a woman [or man] who painstakingly scrubs off her own biological

---

*The norm in our culture is that if someone doesn't smell appealing we will not be attracted to them.*

*Richmond, McCroskey, and Payne, p. 166*

---

scent, dutifully deodorizes her body's every nook and cranny, and then anoints herself with a perfume concocted largely from the musky sex scent of some other, wiser animal."

Of course, we also use odors to make ourselves feel better; after all, we also smell ourselves. And when the smells are pleasant, we feel better about ourselves; when the smells are unpleasant, we feel less good about ourselves and probably (and hopefully) shower and perhaps put on some external scent of cologne.

Aphrodisiacs—or so-called aphrodisiacs—are frequently scents. Amyl nitrate, and its variant butyl nitrate, were recently and frequently used to stimulate sexual arousal. Their possible connection to AIDS, however, has wisely resulted in their discontinuation among most intelligent individuals.

## Messages to Enhance Taste

Smell has long been known to enhance the taste of foods and in fact plays a large part in our enjoyment (or the lack of it) of food generally. Gourmet meals involve great care in the matching of smells from the different foods and wines. Street vendors selling hot dogs, sausages, and similar foods are aided considerably by the smells that penetrate the air and that stimulate the appetite of people who may not have had any intention of eating before they encountered the aroma of sausages, peppers, and onions on the grill.

## Messages to Aid Memory

Some theorists have argued that our sense of smell is the most enduring of all our senses, that our smell memory is the most resistant to loss over time. Whether this extreme position is true or not may be open to debate, but we do know that our memory for smell is quite powerful and we can very easily recall smells from months and even years ago. Similarly, when confronted with a particular smell from our past—for example, we pass a store where bread is being baked, a situation we may have encountered in our childhood—we recognize it easily and we quickly recall the time in our lives when we last experienced that smell.

There is some evidence that smell can aid the learning process. For example, words presented with their accompanying smells, have been found to be remembered better than words presented without smells. Exactly what practical implications will be drawn from this is not clear but it does seem like a most profitable line of research.

## Messages that Aid in Establishing Moods

One of the major advertising lines in selling perfumes and colognes is to associate the smell with the establishment of certain moods. The tone of the ads—whether sensual or athletic, masculine or feminine—echo the implied connection between mood and odor. The ads tell us that this particular scent will elicit the desired response. While the scent itself probably does little to create the mood, our belief in its power probably creates certain behavior which is actually responsible for the mood.

Although the advertising industry undoubtedly exaggerates the effectiveness, there is some research evidence to show that certain smells do have some physiological effects.

## Messages of Identification

Smell enables us to identify (sometimes to misidentify) characteristics of the environment or personal characteristics. Thus, we might be aided in our location of stale water under the sink from the damp, dank smell. At airports, seaports, and similar places, dogs are now used extensively to sniff out cocaine and other illegal substances.

Even illnesses are sometimes signaled by smell. For example, Ruth Winter in her *Smell Book: Scents, Sex, and Society* notes that yellow fever had a "butcher shop" odor, typhoid fever smelled of "freshly baked bread," plague victims smelled of "apples," the skin diseases of eczema and impetigo smelled "moldy," and measles smelled of "freshly plucked feathers." When we experience an upset stomach, our breath frequently takes on a particularly offensive odor which may be aided more by a stomach remedy than by mouth wash.

Manufacturers and advertisers have long-known the importance of smell in selling a product and so put enormous amounts of money into making their products smell "right" and in advertising this "right smell." This is true whether or not the smell has anything to do with the product. For example, many cleaning products such as cleansers and soap powders (and liquids) are given smells that will communicate an image of a "powerful cleaning agent" even though the smell does nothing at all to enhance the cleaning power of the detergent. Advertisers would argue that we actually select detergents largely on the basis of their smells, since they are all approximately equal in their cleaning power. And, as a result, a portion of the purchase price paid by consumers is for the smell that communicates an image but does not assist in the purpose of the detergent. When a positively evaluated smell is firmly associated with a product and when that product becomes identified with that smell, advertisers have achieved a large part of their goal.

# Olfactic Phenomena

As with most sensations, we can discuss smell in terms of a variety of psychophysiological concepts. Here we consider briefly smell blindness, smell adaptation, smell memory, smell overload, smell discrimination, and smell satiation. The first three are adapted from Loretta Malandro and Larry Barker's excellent discussion in *Nonverbal Communication*. These six phenomena should provide added insight into this often neglected nonverbal channel and, more importantly, raise questions about our own use of and reactions to smell.

## Smell Blindness

We all vary in the degree to which we can identify a particular smell and distinguish among smells. Those who are unable to detect smells that others detect readily, suffer from *smell blindness*. Actually, we all suffer from smell blindness to some degree. There is no known remedy to correct this problem other than addressing physiological problems that may be blocking accurate scent detection.

## Smell Adaptation

In much the same way that our eyes gradually adapt to the darkness of a movie house, we also can adapt to smells. *Smell adaptation*, then, refers to the phenomena by which we gradually lose the distinctiveness of a particular smell through repeated association with it. This phenomenon has a positive and a negative side to it. Thus, for example, if placed in a situation in which there is an unpleasant odor, we will soon adapt to it and soon cease to be disturbed by its unpleasantness. The speed with which we adapt, of course, will depend on the strength of the smell; mild smells will be adapted to more quickly than stronger smells. On the other hand, we also quickly adapt to the pleasant smell of cologne (or pizza, if you prefer) and thus soon lose the pleasant sensation we feel upon the first encounter.

## Smell Memory

*Smell memory* refers to our ability to recall previous situations from encountering a particular smell which was associated with the situation. For example, whenever I smell ink, I almost immediately recall elementary school and the ink wells that were built into the desks and the time I was the "ink monitor" and spilled a gallon of ink all over myself.

## Smell Overload

On the analogy of information overload, *smell overload* refers to that phenomenon by which our sense of smell is bombarded by an exceptionally large number or extremely powerful odors. Sometimes we may actually lose (temporarily) our ability to discriminate among or even detect odors we would normally have no difficulty identifying. We might experience this type of effect when an inexperienced cook overseasons food and we lose our ability to distinguish one smell from another.

Sometimes, the bombardment is of the type that simply is so powerful that we continue to smell this odor but lose all the other smells in the environment. We frequently encounter this when someone overdoses with cheap cologne or when we sit next to a particularly foul-smelling cigar. Sometimes, as in the case of the cigar, the smell may function to contaminate the area and ruin it for the use we intended, for example, eating or breathing.

At the very least, in smell overload, we lose our ability to enjoy the variety of smells we might encounter.

## Smell Discrimination

W. S. Cain (1979) reports that people can distinguish hundreds, possibly thousands, of smells. And, it seems, this is an ability that can be improved with training.

Research has found that spouses can identify each other solely through the sense of smell. We learn this smell association for our mate—but also for our dog and for a variety of other people, animals, and things—through frequent association. But, we probably could not describe these smells in any way that would be meaningful to another person.

We can also identify a person's gender from their smell (Schleidt, 1980). More interesting and less obvious, perhaps, is the finding that young siblings were able to correctly identify the t-shirts that were worn by their brothers and sisters on the basis of odor alone (Porter and Moore, 1981).

## Smell Satiation

Smell satiation can be most easily appreciated by looking briefly at its analogue, semantic satiation. When we repeat a word over and over again, that word temporarily loses part of its meaning for us. It quickly returns but for a time, at least, it is lost. Try, for example, saying a word like *elephant* over and over again and you will find that the word suddenly becomes strange, almost foreign, to you. Smell satiation, which occurs in a similar way, is seen when we lose our ability to smell or our ability to identify a smell because of our frequent exposure to it. This phenomenon is seen easily in the heavy smoker who has lost the ability to smell the smoke on his or her clothes. Everyone else can smell it, but the smoker cannot.

# Smell Differences

If you traveled to different parts of the world, especially to parts widely different from your own, you would encounter widely differing smells. Differences in sanitation practices throughout the world account for considerable differences, of course. On the more pleasant side, differences in foods and in the ways in which they are prepared result in great smell differences. Perhaps as a result of these differences, different cultures attribute different meanings to smells. For example, Ruth Winter observes that "Northern Europeans prefer heavier fragrances for use in their cold climes, while Mediterraneans like sophisticated floral smells, probably because they love being surrounded by flowers. Orientals appreciate heavy, spicy, animal perfumes." Although I know of no evidence to support this particular conclusion, we do know that different cultures do have different smell preferences.

Winter also claims that smell preferences differ between men and women as well as between different ages. One representative observation may be used to illustrate this claim: "In the eight- to fourteen-year old group, boys like or tolerate the smell of orange blossoms better than girls do, and young boys show a marked liking for musk lactone, which has sexual associations. The girls in this age group still like almonds but add an inexplicable liking for the tarlike smell of naphthalene."

We are just beginning to understand the role of smell in human communication. Researchers in a wide variety of areas—in physiology, in ethology, in psychology, and in communication—will undoubtedly answer many of the questions we have just suggested here and will surely pose other and more sophisticated questions for the next generation of researchers.

# Smell Communication Exercises

The several exercises included here are designed to heighten your awareness of the role of smell in the communication process. In *Talking about Smells* we explore the difficulty in communicating clearly about smells and the degree of agreement or disagreement among different people in their descriptions of smells. In *Smell Perception* we consider some of the meanings that smell communicates.

In *Thinking about the Effects of Perfume* we examine the findings of a research study investigating the effects of perfume and dress on the way in which men perceived women. The *Observational Record of Smell Communication* should increase your awareness of the forms and functions of communication by smell and its role in the entire field of communication.

# 8.1  Talking About Smells

[Prior to this class, each student should be asked to bring in some object with a unique scent, packaged so as to prevent anyone from learning anything about the object other than its smell.]

For this exercise, the class should be divided into groups of 5 or 6 each. Each member should share the smell he or she has brought to class with the other members who should complete a set of the scales presented below and describe the smell in a few words without consulting with any other group member. [In describing the smell, do not try to name the object from which the smell comes, but rather describe the scent that you perceive.] After the scales have been completed and the smell described, the ratings and the descriptions should be compared for the degree of agreement or disagreement. On what factors was there more agreement? More disagreement? What hypotheses about smell might you advance on the basis of the results obtained from your group? Each group should compile a list of potential hypotheses to be shared with each of the other groups. These hypotheses may be profitably analyzed by trying to adduce evidence and argument—from personal experiences, from the media, from readings—for or against the hypotheses advanced.

Smell No. 1

pleasant _____ : _____ : _____ : _____ : _____ : _____ : _____ unpleasant

high status _____ : _____ : _____ : _____ : _____ : _____ : _____ low status

elegant _____ : _____ : _____ : _____ : _____ : _____ : _____ common

feminine _____ : _____ : _____ : _____ : _____ : _____ : _____ masculine

strong _____ : _____ : _____ : _____ : _____ : _____ : _____ weak

Description:

Smell No. 2

pleasant _____ : _____ : _____ : _____ : _____ : _____ : _____ unpleasant

high status _____ : _____ : _____ : _____ : _____ : _____ : _____ low status

elegant _____ : _____ : _____ : _____ : _____ : _____ : _____ common

feminine _____ : _____ : _____ : _____ : _____ : _____ : _____ masculine

strong _____ : _____ : _____ : _____ : _____ : _____ : _____ weak

Description:

Smell No. 3

pleasant _____ : _____ : _____ : _____ : _____ : _____ : _____ unpleasant

high status _____ : _____ : _____ : _____ : _____ : _____ : _____ low status

elegant _____ : _____ : _____ : _____ : _____ : _____ : _____ common

feminine _____ : _____ : _____ : _____ : _____ : _____ : _____ masculine

strong _____ : _____ : _____ : _____ : _____ : _____ : _____ weak

Description:

Smell No. 4

pleasant _____ : _____ : _____ : _____ : _____ : _____ : _____ unpleasant

high status _____ : _____ : _____ : _____ : _____ : _____ : _____ low status

elegant _____ : _____ : _____ : _____ : _____ : _____ : _____ common

feminine _____ : _____ : _____ : _____ : _____ : _____ : _____ masculine

strong _____ : _____ : _____ : _____ : _____ : _____ : _____ weak

Description:

Smell No. 5

     pleasant _____: _____: _____: _____: _____: _____: _____ unpleasant

high status _____: _____: _____: _____: _____: _____: _____ low status

     elegant _____: _____: _____: _____: _____: _____: _____ common

   feminine _____: _____: _____: _____: _____: _____: _____ masculine

     strong _____: _____: _____: _____: _____: _____: _____ weak

Description:


Smell No. 6

     pleasant _____: _____: _____: _____: _____: _____: _____ unpleasant

high status _____: _____: _____: _____: _____: _____: _____ low status

     elegant _____: _____: _____: _____: _____: _____: _____ common

   feminine _____: _____: _____: _____: _____: _____: _____ masculine

     strong _____: _____: _____: _____: _____: _____: _____ weak

Description:

## 8.2 Smell Perception

This exercise is designed to enable you to explore some of the meanings that scent communicates. For this exercise, each student should complete anonymously the smell perception form presented below. The forms will be collected and read aloud and discussed either in small groups or in the class as a whole. Complete these forms now before reading any further.

In discussing the various smells, consider some or all of the following questions:

1. What types of scents are mentioned most frequently for their messages of attraction? What dimensions are common to these scents?

2. What role does smell play in eating and in the enjoyment of food generally? How does culture figure into this food-smell connection?

3. What role does memory play in the meanings that we attribute to certain smells?

4. What examples can you recall that enabled you to identify characteristics of the environment from smells? Can you recall examples in which you misidentified the smell? Why did this happen?

5. Why is smell important in the selling of a product even when smell has nothing to do with the major purposes of the product, as in cleaning products?

6. How does smell influence our moods and/or emotions?

# Scent Perception Form

Each student should complete this form anonymously. The forms should be collected and discussed either in a group or in the class as a whole.

1.  What smells of other people do you find attractive? What scents do you use to increase other people's attraction to you?

2.  What smells arouse your taste buds? What smells would turn you off to eating?

3.  What smells can you remember from yesterday? What is the earliest smell you can recall?

4.  What would an ideal home smell like? Does your home smell like this? If not, what does it smell like?

5.  What do the following smell like (literally and/or metaphorically)? Describe each one in a brief phrase.

    cheap perfume_____

    cigars _____

    sweat _____

    love _____

    friendship _____

    hate_____

6.  Describe how you feel when you smell the following scents:

    buttered popcorn_____

    the ocean _____

    a dog _____

    after-shave lotion_____

    tar in the street on a hot day _____

# 8.3    Thinking about the Effects of Perfume

In this exercise, try to predict what the experimenters found and then discuss the findings. The experiment was designed to discover the effects of a woman's perfume on how she is perceived by men. Groups were divided as illustrated in the figure presented below.

D  R  E  S  S

|   |   | UP | DOWN |
|---|---|---|---|
| **P** | | | |
| **E** | YES | A | B |
| **R** | | | |
| **F** | | | |
| **U** | | | |
| **M** | NO | C | D |
| **E** | | | |

As you can see the subjects were exposed to four different conditions. In Condition A, the woman was dressed up (stockings, skirt, blouse) and wearing perfume. In Condition B she was dressed down (jeans and sweatshirt) and wearing perfume. In Condition C, she was dressed up and not wearing perfume and in D she was dressed down and not wearing perfume.

In all cases, they talked with a woman. They were then asked to indicate the degree to which they thought the woman attractive and the degree to which they liked the woman. Under which condition was the woman thought most attractive? Under which condition was the woman liked the most? Before reading the results, try to predict what you think would occur. What reasons can you advance to support your prediction?

---

It was found (see J. C. Horn, "The Scentimental Perfume Put-Off," *Psychology Today* (May 1980):12, 16) that the men liked most and thought most attractive the women who dressed down and wore perfume and liked least and thought least attractive the woman who dressed up and wore perfume.

# 8.4  Observational Record of Smell Communication

This observational record form is designed to increase your awareness of the forms and functions of communication by smell and its role in the total communication act.

**Part One. Olfactic Phenomena**

Provide examples of the following:

Smell Blindness

Smell Adaptation

Smell Memory

Smell Overload

Smell Discrimination

Smell Satiation

**Part Two. Smell in Interpersonal Interactions**

Select a sample of 10 people and try to answer (in a preliminary way) one of the following questions:

1. Do men prefer interacting with women who are or who aren't wearing perfume or cologne?

2. Do women prefer interacting with men who are or who aren't wearing after-shave lotion or cologne?

3. Do men prefer interacting with other men who are or who aren't wearing after-shave lotion or cologne?

4. Do women prefer interacting with other women who are or who aren't wearing perfume or cologne?

**Part Three. The Role of Smell in Marketing**

Go through a supermarket and record as many examples as you can find to demonstrate the usage of nonfunctional scent (a product whose function is unrelated to the way it smells) in selling and in marketing products. Create a chart similar to the one presented here:

Product                                 Smell Promised

1.                                       1.

2.                                       2.

3.                                       3.

4.                                       4.

5.                                       5.

# Review and Discussion Questions

1. Define olfactics. How important do you think olfactics is to the study of communication in general and to the study of nonverbal communication in particular?

2. Five types of messages that smell communicates are identified in this chapter: attraction, enhance taste, aid memory, aid in mood creation, and identification. Provide one example of each type of message that smell has communicated in your own experience. Are there other messages that smell communicates that cannot be subsumed under any of these five headings? Explain.

3. Describe any gender differences that you think exist in regard to smell communication. Consider men and women as both senders and receivers of smell messages.

4. Provide at least one example to illustrate the olfactory phenomena of smell blindness, smell adaptation, smell memory, smell overload, smell discrimination, and smell satiation.

5. Total the amount of money you spend in one year on perfumes, colognes, after shave lotions, room and car odorizers, and any other scents. Compare this to the amount of money you contribute to charity, spend on newspapers and news magazines, and spend on books. Any surprises?

# Terms to Define

Olfaction/Olfactics

Smell Blindness

Smell Adaptation

Smell Memory

Smell Overload

Smell Discrimination

Smell Satiation

Additional relevant terms in olfactic communication

# 9

# Temporal Communication (Chronemics)

**Chapter Outline**

## Objectives

After completing this chapter, you should be able to:

1. define *chronemics*
2. explain the nature of cultural time, psychological time, and biological time
3. distinguish among technical time, formal time, and informal time
4. distinguish between displaced and diffused time orientations
5. distinguish among past, present, and future orientations and identify some of the psychological differences that have been found
6. define *biorhythms* and explain the nature of the physical, emotional, and intellectual cycles

Temporal or time communication, more formally called chronemics, deals with the communicative dimension of time. How we use time, how we organize time, how we react to time, the messages that different times communicate, the meanings we derive from the use of time by others, the time preferences we have, the ways in which our culture divides up time, and the ways in which our biological clocks operate are some of the topics normally covered in chronemics.

Generally, three areas of time communication are distinguished.

> Chronemics is concerned with how we use and structure time. It is a significant area of nonverbal communication because we generally perceive our actions and reactions on the basis of a time sequence. We talk about what we will do tomorrow, what we should have done yesterday, how we have wasted time.
>
> Hickson and Stacks, p. 122

# Cultural Time

Cultural time is concerned with how the culture in which we were raised and in which we now live treats time. Three types of cultural time are identified.

## Technical Time

Technical time refers to precise, scientific time. It is the definition of the atomic year as 365 days, 5 hours, 48 minutes, and 45.51 seconds. It is the milliseconds of the scientific researcher. This is the least interesting aspect of time in terms of communication simply because we rarely operate on this level.

## Formal Time

Formal time refers to the manner in which a culture defines and teaches time. Here we define time in terms of seconds, minutes, hours, days, weeks, months, years, and centuries. All of these divisions are relatively arbitrary; other cultures may divide up time in very different ways, for example, according to phases of the moon or the seasons for various crops.

But, formal time is seen more clearly in, for example, the way in which we create time blocks for different purposes. For example, we allot four years for high school and four years for college. We further divide up the college years into semesters or quarters and we quite arbitrarily assign hours and credits to various academic subjects. Thus, for example, we assign three credits for forty-five hours of class. Further, we say that 128 credits or approximately 43 forty-five hour classes are required for a college degree.

Similarly, the media divides up time into 30 minute and 60 minute blocks. Advertisers divide media time into 15 second, 30 second, and 60 second commercial spots. All these are arbitrary divisions of time. Whatever naturalness we may perceive or feel is due to the familiarity of these time divisions.

## Informal Time

Informal time refers to the rather loose use of time terms such as *forever, immediately, soon, right away, early, not too late*, and *in a few minutes*. These terms create the most difficulties because they are usually interpreted so differently by different people. To the teenager, *early* may mean 1 a.m. whereas to the teen's parents, it may mean 11 p.m.

## Displaced and Diffused Time Orientations

In addition to our orientation to past, present, or future time we may also look at our time orientations in terms of their being displaced or diffused. A displaced time orientation views time exactly and precisely. A person with this orientation views an appointment at 5 p.m. to mean exactly that: 5 p.m. A person with a diffused time orientation, however, views time approximately. An appointment for

5 p.m. means that one should arrive sometime around 5 p.m., say between 4 p.m. and 6 p.m.

Entire cultures may also be characterized as treating time as displaced or diffused. In some cultures—Japan is a good example— time is displaced, things are done exactly on time. In other cultures— Indonesia is a good example—time is diffused, things are done on an approximate, loose time schedule. In fact, when researchers compared the accuracy of the clocks in Japan, Indonesia, the United States, Italy, England, and Taiwan, they found that the clocks were most accurate in Japan and least accurate in Indonesia. Interestingly enough, when the speed with which citizens of these countries walk was measured, it was found that the Japanese walked the fastest, the Indonesians the slowest.

---

Perhaps more than any other culture the North American culture is time conscious. Look around you. Regardless of where you go you will find a clock or some type of time keeper. We have clocks in our desk calendars, in our bathrooms, in our bedrooms, in our kitchens, in our classrooms, in our work places, in our pens and pencils, in our calculators; in our rings, in our necklaces, in our belt buckles, in our earrings, in our money clips, in our computers, in our cards, on our desks, in our radios, TVs, VCRs and even in our exercise equipment. No other culture in the world lets time rule it as we do.

Richmond, McCroskey, and Payne, p. 172

---

# Psychological Time

Psychological time refers to the importance we place on the past, the present, and the future.

## Past Orientation

Persons (and entire cultures) who emphasize the past often look to the past for guidance in the present; they frequently apply old methods to present ideas. They frequently relive old times and long for "the good old days."

## Present Orientation

Persons who emphasize the present are often oriented to deriving their satisfactions immediately. These people live in the present, without reverence for the past or worry for the future. The present activity is what commands attention and is engaged in not for its future rewards or its past history but because it is happening now.

A present-orientation (sometimes called present-day living) is valuable because it enables us to enjoy what is going on now. It allows us the fullest enjoyment of each moment. On the other hand, a present-orientation that ignores the past and the future and that concentrates solely on the pleasures of the moment can create serious problems. It may hinder our planning and preparing for the inevitable future and may also lead us to forget or to ignore our history, a history that influences the present in numerous and significant ways.

## Future Orientation

Persons who emphasize the future work in the present to achieve future rewards and benefits. Most students, for example, attend college in order to attain future rewards, a better job, a high salary, a more comfortable style of living, and so on.

Of course, these three divisions are drawn here in bold relief. Most of us are a combination of all three psychological time orientations. Yet, if we look carefully at ourselves, we would probably find that one time orientation dominates our family's life and our own life as well.

# Biological Time

Biological time orientation often refers to our body clocks, the ways in which our bodies respond to different times. One popular approach to biological time is that of biorhythms. According to biorhythm research, we function in three different cycles. Each cycle begins at birth and continues throughout life, repeating itself periodically. Each cycle has an up-side, during which we are particularly sharp, a down-side, during which we are particularly dull, and a crucial period during which we are at our absolute worst. The three cycles are physical, emotional, and intellectual.

## The Physical Cycle

The physical cycle lasts 23 days and is concerned with strength, energy, coordination, resistance to disease. During the up-side we are in good health, we have coordinated balance, we are hyperactive, and are especially good athletically. During the down-side we are tired and lazy, we lack coordination, we have low endurance, and we are especially prone to accidents and ailments.

## The Emotional Cycle

The emotional cycle lasts 28 days and is concerned with mood, our optimism and pessimism, and our ability to work effectively with others. During the up-side we are calm, cheerful, cooperative, understanding, and creative. During the down-side, we are moody, negative, irritable, and hypersensitive.

## The Intellectual Cycle

The intellectual cycle lasts 33 days and is concerned with our intellectual abilities and activities. During the up-side we are intellectually driven and efficient, we have good memory power and can make rapid and accurate decisions. During the down-side our thinking capacity is diminished, our mental abilities are low, our memory is poor, and our reactions are slower.

There is, unfortunately, little substantial research to substantiate the claims made by proponents of biorhythmic analysis. Nevertheless, it does raise the important issue of body clock cycles and how these may influence our behaviors, moods, and abilities. The exercise, *Biorhythms*, shows you how you can compute your own biorhythms.

# Temporal Communication Exercises

The *Workbook* exercises are designed to enable you to analyze your own time orientations in at least two different ways, to consider the influence of time, and to heighten your awareness of how rules of time operate in our society. In *Talking about Time* you are asked to examine our various cultural values concerning time as they are expressed in a wide variety of clichés. *The Psychological Time Test* will enable you to analyze your own time preferences and, most important, to explore some of the implications of these preferences. It has been demonstrated that time preference or orientation will have a great influence on, for example, one's future success and financial status.

The *Biorhythm* exercise will enable you to calculate your own biorhythms so that you might see for yourself if the claims made have any validity for you. Specific directions are provided for calculating your physical, emotional, and intellectual cycles. Last, the *Rules of Temporal Communication* exercise is designed to increase your awareness of the rule-governed nature of time, for example, how these rules differ from one subculture to another and what adherence to or violation of these rules communicates about you.

# 9.1  Talking About Time

The purpose of this brief exercise is to explore some of our cultural values concerning time as well as our own thoughts and feelings about time. Below are presented some commonly heard observations about time. Most of these were originally considered clever but, through overuse, have become trite and would now be considered clichés. Because of this overuse, they are particularly well-suited for examining a culture's views and our own thoughts concerning time. Read each of the clichés presented below and, for each, identify:

1. *the meaning expressed in each of these expressions.* For example, in the expression, "better late than never," the meaning is that it is more important that something is done than when it is done. It is better to do something late than not at all. Further, being late is no excuse for not doing something. However, the expression is frequently used as an excuse for lateness.

2. *the cultural value expressed in these observations; the importance of this value in your particular culture or subculture.* For example, in "better late than never," the cultural value seems to be the primary importance of getting things done, of accomplishing something.

3. *one situation in which the expression would hold true and one situation in which the expression would prove false.* For example, "better late than never" would probably hold true for saving money or for cleaning the house or for reading that book we postponed so many times. The expression might prove false if the situation concerned confessing our love after our beloved was happily married with four children.

**Time Expressions**

1. Bide your time.
2. A bird in the hand is worth two in the bush.
3. Every dog has its day.
4. He who hesitates is lost.
5. Time heals all wounds.
6. A stitch in time saves nine.
7. Time will tell.
8. There's a time for everything.
9. Time is money.
10. Time waits for no one.
11. Procrastination is the thief of time.
12. Punctuality is the thief of time.

# 9.2 The Psychological Time Test*

**Instructions:** For each statement, indicate whether the statement is TRUE (T) for your general attitude and behavior or UNTRUE (F) for your general attitude and behavior.

_____ 1. Meeting tomorrow's deadlines and doing other necessary work comes before tonight's partying.

_____ 2. I meet my obligations to friends and authorities on time.

_____ 3. I complete projects on time by making steady progress.

_____ 4. I am able to resist temptations when I know there is work to be done.

_____ 5. I keep working at a difficult, uninteresting task if it will help me get ahead.

_____ 6. If things don't get done on time, I don't worry about it.

_____ 7. I think that it's useless to plan too far ahead because things hardly ever come out the way you planned anyway.

_____ 8. I try to live one day at a time.

_____ 9. I live to make better what *is* rather than to be concerned about what *will be*.

_____ 10. It seems to me that it doesn't make sense to worry about the future, since fate determines whatever will be, will be.

_____ 11. I believe that getting together with friends to party is one of life's important pleasures.

_____ 12. I do things impulsively, making decisions on the spur of the moment.

_____ 13. I take risks to put excitement in my life.

_____ 14. I get drunk at parties.

_____ 15. It's fun to gamble.

_____ 16. Thinking about the future is pleasant to me.

_____ 17. When I want to achieve something, I set subgoals and consider specific means for reaching those goals.

_____ 18. It seems to me that my career path is pretty well laid out.

_____ 19. It upsets me to be late for appointments.

_____ 20. I meet my obligations to friends and authorities on time.

_____ 21. I get irritated at people who keep me waiting when we've agreed to meet at a given time.

_____ 22. It makes sense to invest a substantial part of my income in insurance premiums.

_____ 23. I believe that "A stitch in time saves nine."

_____ 24. I believe the "A bird in the hand is worth two in the bush."

_____ 25. I believe it is important to save for a rainy day.

_____ 26. I believe a person's day should be planned each morning.

_____ 27. I make lists of things I must do.

_____ 28. When I want to achieve something, I set subgoals and consider specific means for reaching those goals.

_____ 29. I believe that "A stitch in time saves nine."

This psychological time test measures seven different factors. If you scored True for all or most of the questions within any given factor, then you are probably high on that factor; if you scored False for all or most of the questions within any given factor, then you are probably low on that factor.

1. The first factor, measured by questions 1-5, is a future, work motivation, perseverance orientation. These people have a strong work ethic and are committed to completing a task despite difficulties and temptations.

2. The second factor, measured by questions 6-10, is a present, fatalistic, worry-free orientation. People who score high on this factor live one day at a time, not necessarily to enjoy the day but to avoid planning for the next day and to avoid the anxiety about a future that seems determined by fate rather than by anything they can do themselves.

3. The third factor, measured by questions 11-15, is a present, hedonistic, pleasure-seeking, partying orientation. These people seek to enjoy the present, take risks and engage in a variety of impulsive actions. Teenagers score particularly high on this factor.

4. The fourth factor, measured by questions 16-18, is a future, goal seeking and planning orientation. These people derive special pleasure from planning and achieving a variety of goals.

5. The fifth factor, measured by questions 19-21, is a time sensitivity orientation. People who score high on this factor are especially sensitive to time and its role in social obligations.

6. The sixth factor, measured by questions 22-25, is a future, pragmatic action orientation. These people do what they have to do to achieve the future they want. They take practical actions for future gain.

7. The seventh factor, measured by questions 26-29, is a future, somewhat obsessive daily planning orientation. People who score high on this factor make daily "to do" lists, devote great attention to specific details and subordinate goals.

Among the findings relevant to psychological time orientation are these:

1. Future income is positively related to future orientation. The more future oriented a person is, the greater that person's income is likely to be. Present orientation is strongest among lowest income males.

2. Men are more hedonistic than women, regardless of their income level.

3. The time orientation that people develop depends a great deal on their socioeconomic class and their personal experiences. Gonzalez and Zimbardo, who developed this scale and upon whose research these findings are based, observe: "A child with parents in unskilled and semiskilled occupations is usually socialized in a way that promotes a present-oriented fatalism and hedonism. A child of parents who are managers, teachers or other professionals learns future-oriented values and strategies designed to promote achievement."

4. Different time perspectives also account for much intercultural misunderstanding since different cultures will often teach their members drastically different time orientations. The future-oriented person who works for tomorrow's goals will frequently look down upon the present-oriented person who avoids planning for tomorrow and focuses on enjoying today as lazy and poorly motivated. In turn, the present-oriented person may see those with strong future orientations as obsessed with accumulating wealth or rising in status.

[For additional information on this psychological time test see Alexander Gonzalez and Philip G. Zimbardo, "Time in Perspective," *Psychology Today* 19 (March 1985:21-26.]

*This test was constructed by Alexander Gonzalez and Philip G. Zimbardo, "Time in Perspective," *Psychology Today* 19 (March 1985):20-26. The test is reprinted by permission of Alexander Gonzalez and Philip Zimbardo.

# 9.3 Biorhythms

**Directions for Computing Biorhythms**

1. Calculate the number of days you have lived up to and including today but not including your birthdate:
    a. Multiply 365 by your age.
    b. Add any leap year days (February 29th); leap years were: 1988, 1984, 1980, 1976, 1972, 1968, 1964, 1960, 1956, 1952, 1948, 1944, 1940.
    c. Add the number of days you have lived from your last birthday.

*To calculate your 23-day physical cycle:*

2. Divide the total number of days you have lived by 23.
3. Multiply the quotient whole number by 23.
4. Subtract the product (from Step 3) from the total number of days lived to obtain the number of days you are into your present physical cycle.
5. Compute the midpoint of your cycle.
    a. Mark the beginning point of the physical cycle by counting backwards (from today) the number of days you are into your present cycle.
    b. Count forward from this beginning point 11½ days.
6. Draw a curve of your physical cycle:
    a. If you are in the first half of your cycle (that is, if the number of days you are into this cycle is less than 11½), then draw your curve from the positive (upper half) part of the graph through the midpoint to the negative (lower half) part of the graph.
    b. If you are in the second half of your cycle (that is, if the number of days you are into your cycle is greater than 11½) then draw your curve from the negative (lower half) part of the graph through the midpoint to the positive (upper half) part of the graph.
    c. Each 11½ days the curve should cross the baseline going from positive to negative or from negative to positive.

*To calculate your 28-day sensitivity cycle:*

7. Divide the total number of days you have lived by 28.
8. Multiply the quotient whole number by 28.
9. Subtract the product (from Step 8) from the total number of days you have lived to obtain the number of days you are into your sensitivity cycle.
10. Compute the midpoint of your sensitivity cycle:
    a. Mark the beginning point of the sensitivity cycle by counting backwards (from today) the number of days you are into your present sensitivity cycle.
    b. Count forward 14 days for the midpoint of this cycle.
11. Draw a curve of your sensitivity cycle by following the directions in Step 6 but using 14 instead of 11½ since the sensitivity cycle is 28 days (28/2 = 14).

*To calculate your 33-day intellectual cycle:*

12. Divide the total number of days you have lived by 33.

13. Multiply the quotient whole number by 33.

14. Subtract the product (from Step 13) from the total number of days you have lived to obtain the number of days you are into your intellectual cycle.

15. Compute the midpoint of your intellectual cycle:

    a. Mark the beginning point of your intellectual cycle by counting backwards (from today) the number of days you are into your present intellectual cycle.

    b. Count forward 16½ days to obtain the midpoint of your intellectual cycle.

16. Draw a curve of your intellectual cycle by following the directions in Step 6 but using 16½ instead of 11½ since the intellectual cycle is 33 days (33/2 = 16½).

*An Example of Biorhythm Calculation*

1. 365 x 47 = 17155
   + 12 leap years = 17167
   + 163 days = 17330 = total days lived (as of January 11, 1986)

2. 17330/23 = 753 cycles

3. 753 x 23 = 17319

4. 17330-17319 = 11 (I'm 11 days into my 754th physical cycle)

5. January 1 = the start of physical cycle since today is the 11th and I'm 11 days into my physical cycle. Between the 11th and the 12th of January = midpoint of physical cycle.

6.

| 1 | 2 | 3 | 4 | 5 | 6 | 7 | 8 | 9 | 10 | 11 | 12 | 13 | 14 | 15 | 16 | 17 | 18 | 19 | 20 | 21 | 22 | 23 | 24 | 25 | 26 | 27 | 28 | 29 | 30 | 31 | 1 | 2 | 3 | 4 | 5 | 6 | 7 | 8 | 9 |

January                                                                                    February

7. 17330/28 = 618

8. 28 x 618 = 17304

9. 17330 − 17304 = 26 = the number of days I'm into my present sensitivity cycle.

10. Beginning of sensitivity cycle was December 17th (this is 26 days prior to January 11). Counting forward 14 days, will put the midpoint of my sensitivity cycle at December 30th.

11.

| 1 | 2 | 3 | 4 | 5 | 6 | 7 | 8 | 9 | 10 | 11 | 12 | 13 | 14 | 15 | 16 | 17 | 18 | 19 | 20 | 21 | 22 | 23 | 24 | 25 | 26 | 27 | 28 | 29 | 30 | 31 | 1 | 2 | 3 | 4 | 5 | 6 | 7 | 8 | 9 |

January                                                                                    February

12. 17330/33 = 525

13. 525 x 33 = 17325

14. 17330 − 17325 = 5 (I'm 5 days into my present intellectual cycle)

15. Midpoint of intellectual cycle = January 7th. Counting forward 16½ days would put the midpoint of my intellectual cycle at between the 22nd and 23rd of January.

16.

| 1 | 2 | 3 | 4 | 5 | 6 | 7 | 8 | 9 | 10 | 11 | 12 | 13 | 14 | 15 | 16 | 17 | 18 | 19 | 20 | 21 | 22 | 23 | 24 | 25 | 26 | 27 | 28 | 29 | 30 | 31 | 1 | 2 | 3 | 4 | 5 | 6 | 7 | 8 | 9 |

January                                                                        February

### 1989

**January**

| S | M | T | W | T | F | S |
|---|---|---|---|---|---|---|
| 1 | 2 | 3 | 4 | 5 | 6 | 7 |
| 8 | 9 | 10 | 11 | 12 | 13 | 14 |
| 15 | 16 | 17 | 18 | 19 | 20 | 21 |
| 22 | 23 | 24 | 25 | 26 | 27 | 28 |
| 29 | 30 | 31 | | | | |

**February**

| S | M | T | W | T | F | S |
|---|---|---|---|---|---|---|
| | | | 1 | 2 | 3 | 4 |
| 5 | 6 | 7 | 8 | 9 | 10 | 11 |
| 12 | 13 | 14 | 15 | 16 | 17 | 18 |
| 19 | 20 | 21 | 22 | 23 | 24 | 25 |
| 26 | 27 | 28 | | | | |

**March**

| S | M | T | W | T | F | S |
|---|---|---|---|---|---|---|
| | | | 1 | 2 | 3 | 4 |
| 5 | 6 | 7 | 8 | 9 | 10 | 11 |
| 12 | 13 | 14 | 15 | 16 | 17 | 18 |
| 19 | 20 | 21 | 22 | 23 | 24 | 25 |
| 26 | 27 | 28 | 29 | 30 | 31 | |

**April**

| S | M | T | W | T | F | S |
|---|---|---|---|---|---|---|
| | | | | | | 1 |
| 2 | 3 | 4 | 5 | 6 | 7 | 8 |
| 9 | 10 | 11 | 12 | 13 | 14 | 15 |
| 16 | 17 | 18 | 19 | 20 | 21 | 22 |
| 23 | 24 | 25 | 26 | 27 | 28 | 29 |
| 30 | | | | | | |

**May**

| S | M | T | W | T | F | S |
|---|---|---|---|---|---|---|
| | 1 | 2 | 3 | 4 | 5 | 6 |
| 7 | 8 | 9 | 10 | 11 | 12 | 13 |
| 14 | 15 | 16 | 17 | 18 | 19 | 20 |
| 21 | 22 | 23 | 24 | 25 | 26 | 27 |
| 28 | 29 | 30 | 31 | | | |

**June**

| S | M | T | W | T | F | S |
|---|---|---|---|---|---|---|
| | | | | 1 | 2 | 3 |
| 4 | 5 | 6 | 7 | 8 | 9 | 10 |
| 11 | 12 | 13 | 14 | 15 | 16 | 17 |
| 18 | 19 | 20 | 21 | 22 | 23 | 24 |
| 25 | 26 | 27 | 28 | 29 | 30 | |

**July**

| S | M | T | W | T | F | S |
|---|---|---|---|---|---|---|
| | | | | | | 1 |
| 2 | 3 | 4 | 5 | 6 | 7 | 8 |
| 9 | 10 | 11 | 12 | 13 | 14 | 15 |
| 16 | 17 | 18 | 19 | 20 | 21 | 22 |
| 23 | 24 | 25 | 26 | 27 | 28 | 29 |
| 30 | 31 | | | | | |

**August**

| S | M | T | W | T | F | S |
|---|---|---|---|---|---|---|
| | | 1 | 2 | 3 | 4 | 5 |
| 6 | 7 | 8 | 9 | 10 | 11 | 12 |
| 13 | 14 | 15 | 16 | 17 | 18 | 19 |
| 20 | 21 | 22 | 23 | 24 | 25 | 26 |
| 27 | 28 | 29 | 30 | 31 | | |

**September**

| S | M | T | W | T | F | S |
|---|---|---|---|---|---|---|
| | | | | | 1 | 2 |
| 3 | 4 | 5 | 6 | 7 | 8 | 9 |
| 10 | 11 | 12 | 13 | 14 | 15 | 16 |
| 17 | 18 | 19 | 20 | 21 | 22 | 23 |
| 24 | 25 | 26 | 27 | 28 | 29 | 30 |

**October**

| S | M | T | W | T | F | S |
|---|---|---|---|---|---|---|
| 1 | 2 | 3 | 4 | 5 | 6 | 7 |
| 8 | 9 | 10 | 11 | 12 | 13 | 14 |
| 15 | 16 | 17 | 18 | 19 | 20 | 21 |
| 22 | 23 | 24 | 25 | 26 | 27 | 28 |
| 29 | 30 | 31 | | | | |

**November**

| S | M | T | W | T | F | S |
|---|---|---|---|---|---|---|
| | | | 1 | 2 | 3 | 4 |
| 5 | 6 | 7 | 8 | 9 | 10 | 11 |
| 12 | 13 | 14 | 15 | 16 | 17 | 18 |
| 19 | 20 | 21 | 22 | 23 | 24 | 25 |
| 26 | 27 | 28 | 29 | 30 | | |

**December**

| S | M | T | W | T | F | S |
|---|---|---|---|---|---|---|
| | | | | | 1 | 2 |
| 3 | 4 | 5 | 6 | 7 | 8 | 9 |
| 10 | 11 | 12 | 13 | 14 | 15 | 16 |
| 17 | 18 | 19 | 20 | 21 | 22 | 23 |
| 24 | 25 | 26 | 27 | 28 | 29 | 30 |
| 31 | | | | | | |

### 1990

**January**

| S | M | T | W | T | F | S |
|---|---|---|---|---|---|---|
| | 1 | 2 | 3 | 4 | 5 | 6 |
| 7 | 8 | 9 | 10 | 11 | 12 | 13 |
| 14 | 15 | 16 | 17 | 18 | 19 | 20 |
| 21 | 22 | 23 | 24 | 25 | 26 | 27 |
| 28 | 29 | 30 | 31 | | | |

**February**

| S | M | T | W | T | F | S |
|---|---|---|---|---|---|---|
| | | | | 1 | 2 | 3 |
| 4 | 5 | 6 | 7 | 8 | 9 | 10 |
| 11 | 12 | 13 | 14 | 15 | 16 | 17 |
| 18 | 19 | 20 | 21 | 22 | 23 | 24 |
| 25 | 26 | 27 | 28 | | | |

**March**

| S | M | T | W | T | F | S |
|---|---|---|---|---|---|---|
| | | | | 1 | 2 | 3 |
| 4 | 5 | 6 | 7 | 8 | 9 | 10 |
| 11 | 12 | 13 | 14 | 15 | 16 | 17 |
| 18 | 19 | 20 | 21 | 22 | 23 | 24 |
| 25 | 26 | 27 | 28 | 29 | 30 | 31 |

**April**

| S | M | T | W | T | F | S |
|---|---|---|---|---|---|---|
| 1 | 2 | 3 | 4 | 5 | 6 | 7 |
| 8 | 9 | 10 | 11 | 12 | 13 | 14 |
| 15 | 16 | 17 | 18 | 19 | 20 | 21 |
| 22 | 23 | 24 | 25 | 26 | 27 | 28 |
| 29 | 30 | | | | | |

**May**

| S | M | T | W | T | F | S |
|---|---|---|---|---|---|---|
| | | 1 | 2 | 3 | 4 | 5 |
| 6 | 7 | 8 | 9 | 10 | 11 | 12 |
| 13 | 14 | 15 | 16 | 17 | 18 | 19 |
| 20 | 21 | 22 | 23 | 24 | 25 | 26 |
| 27 | 28 | 29 | 30 | 31 | | |

**June**

| S | M | T | W | T | F | S |
|---|---|---|---|---|---|---|
| | | | | | 1 | 2 |
| 3 | 4 | 5 | 6 | 7 | 8 | 9 |
| 10 | 11 | 12 | 13 | 14 | 15 | 16 |
| 17 | 18 | 19 | 20 | 21 | 22 | 23 |
| 24 | 25 | 26 | 27 | 28 | 29 | 30 |

**July**

| S | M | T | W | T | F | S |
|---|---|---|---|---|---|---|
| 1 | 2 | 3 | 4 | 5 | 6 | 7 |
| 8 | 9 | 10 | 11 | 12 | 13 | 14 |
| 15 | 16 | 17 | 18 | 19 | 20 | 21 |
| 22 | 23 | 24 | 25 | 26 | 27 | 28 |
| 29 | 30 | 31 | | | | |

**August**

| S | M | T | W | T | F | S |
|---|---|---|---|---|---|---|
| | | | 1 | 2 | 3 | 4 |
| 5 | 6 | 7 | 8 | 9 | 10 | 11 |
| 12 | 13 | 14 | 15 | 16 | 17 | 18 |
| 19 | 20 | 21 | 22 | 23 | 24 | 25 |
| 26 | 27 | 28 | 29 | 30 | 31 | |

**September**

| S | M | T | W | T | F | S |
|---|---|---|---|---|---|---|
| | | | | | | 1 |
| 2 | 3 | 4 | 5 | 6 | 7 | 8 |
| 9 | 10 | 11 | 12 | 13 | 14 | 15 |
| 16 | 17 | 18 | 19 | 20 | 21 | 22 |
| 23 | 24 | 25 | 26 | 27 | 28 | 29 |
| 30 | | | | | | |

**October**

| S | M | T | W | T | F | S |
|---|---|---|---|---|---|---|
| | 1 | 2 | 3 | 4 | 5 | 6 |
| 7 | 8 | 9 | 10 | 11 | 12 | 13 |
| 14 | 15 | 16 | 17 | 18 | 19 | 20 |
| 21 | 22 | 23 | 24 | 25 | 26 | 27 |
| 28 | 29 | 30 | 31 | | | |

**November**

| S | M | T | W | T | F | S |
|---|---|---|---|---|---|---|
| | | | | 1 | 2 | 3 |
| 4 | 5 | 6 | 7 | 8 | 9 | 10 |
| 11 | 12 | 13 | 14 | 15 | 16 | 17 |
| 18 | 19 | 20 | 21 | 22 | 23 | 24 |
| 25 | 26 | 27 | 28 | 29 | 30 | |

**December**

| S | M | T | W | T | F | S |
|---|---|---|---|---|---|---|
| | | | | | | 1 |
| 2 | 3 | 4 | 5 | 6 | 7 | 8 |
| 9 | 10 | 11 | 12 | 13 | 14 | 15 |
| 16 | 17 | 18 | 19 | 20 | 21 | 22 |
| 23 | 24 | 25 | 26 | 27 | 28 | 29 |
| 30 | 31 | | | | | |

## 1991

### January
| S | M | T | W | T | F | S |
|---|---|---|---|---|---|---|
|   |   | 1 | 2 | 3 | 4 | 5 |
| 6 | 7 | 8 | 9 | 10 | 11 | 12 |
| 13 | 14 | 15 | 16 | 17 | 18 | 19 |
| 20 | 21 | 22 | 23 | 24 | 25 | 26 |
| 27 | 28 | 29 | 30 | 31 |   |   |

### February
| S | M | T | W | T | F | S |
|---|---|---|---|---|---|---|
|   |   |   |   |   | 1 | 2 |
| 3 | 4 | 5 | 6 | 7 | 8 | 9 |
| 10 | 11 | 12 | 13 | 14 | 15 | 16 |
| 17 | 18 | 19 | 20 | 21 | 22 | 23 |
| 24 | 25 | 26 | 27 | 28 |   |   |

### March
| S | M | T | W | T | F | S |
|---|---|---|---|---|---|---|
|   |   |   |   |   | 1 | 2 |
| 3 | 4 | 5 | 6 | 7 | 8 | 9 |
| 10 | 11 | 12 | 13 | 14 | 15 | 16 |
| 17 | 18 | 19 | 20 | 21 | 22 | 23 |
| 24 | 25 | 26 | 27 | 28 | 29 | 30 |
| 31 |   |   |   |   |   |   |

### April
| S | M | T | W | T | F | S |
|---|---|---|---|---|---|---|
|   | 1 | 2 | 3 | 4 | 5 | 6 |
| 7 | 8 | 9 | 10 | 11 | 12 | 13 |
| 14 | 15 | 16 | 17 | 18 | 19 | 20 |
| 21 | 22 | 23 | 24 | 25 | 26 | 27 |
| 28 | 29 | 30 |   |   |   |   |

### May
| S | M | T | W | T | F | S |
|---|---|---|---|---|---|---|
|   |   |   | 1 | 2 | 3 | 4 |
| 5 | 6 | 7 | 8 | 9 | 10 | 11 |
| 12 | 13 | 14 | 15 | 16 | 17 | 18 |
| 19 | 20 | 21 | 22 | 23 | 24 | 25 |
| 26 | 27 | 28 | 29 | 30 | 31 |   |

### June
| S | M | T | W | T | F | S |
|---|---|---|---|---|---|---|
|   |   |   |   |   |   | 1 |
| 2 | 3 | 4 | 5 | 6 | 7 | 8 |
| 9 | 10 | 11 | 12 | 13 | 14 | 15 |
| 16 | 17 | 18 | 19 | 20 | 21 | 22 |
| 23 | 24 | 25 | 26 | 27 | 28 | 29 |
| 30 |   |   |   |   |   |   |

### July
| S | M | T | W | T | F | S |
|---|---|---|---|---|---|---|
|   | 1 | 2 | 3 | 4 | 5 | 6 |
| 7 | 8 | 9 | 10 | 11 | 12 | 13 |
| 14 | 15 | 16 | 17 | 18 | 19 | 20 |
| 21 | 22 | 23 | 24 | 25 | 26 | 27 |
| 28 | 29 | 30 | 31 |   |   |   |

### August
| S | M | T | W | T | F | S |
|---|---|---|---|---|---|---|
|   |   |   |   | 1 | 2 | 3 |
| 4 | 5 | 6 | 7 | 8 | 9 | 10 |
| 11 | 12 | 13 | 14 | 15 | 16 | 17 |
| 18 | 19 | 20 | 21 | 22 | 23 | 24 |
| 25 | 26 | 27 | 28 | 29 | 30 | 31 |

### September
| S | M | T | W | T | F | S |
|---|---|---|---|---|---|---|
| 1 | 2 | 3 | 4 | 5 | 6 | 7 |
| 8 | 9 | 10 | 11 | 12 | 13 | 14 |
| 15 | 16 | 17 | 18 | 19 | 20 | 21 |
| 22 | 23 | 24 | 25 | 26 | 27 | 28 |
| 29 | 30 |   |   |   |   |   |

### October
| S | M | T | W | T | F | S |
|---|---|---|---|---|---|---|
|   |   | 1 | 2 | 3 | 4 | 5 |
| 6 | 7 | 8 | 9 | 10 | 11 | 12 |
| 13 | 14 | 15 | 16 | 17 | 18 | 19 |
| 20 | 21 | 22 | 23 | 24 | 25 | 26 |
| 27 | 28 | 29 | 30 | 31 |   |   |

### November
| S | M | T | W | T | F | S |
|---|---|---|---|---|---|---|
|   |   |   |   |   | 1 | 2 |
| 3 | 4 | 5 | 6 | 7 | 8 | 9 |
| 10 | 11 | 12 | 13 | 14 | 15 | 16 |
| 17 | 18 | 19 | 20 | 21 | 22 | 23 |
| 24 | 25 | 26 | 27 | 28 | 29 | 30 |

### December
| S | M | T | W | T | F | S |
|---|---|---|---|---|---|---|
| 1 | 2 | 3 | 4 | 5 | 6 | 7 |
| 8 | 9 | 10 | 11 | 12 | 13 | 14 |
| 15 | 16 | 17 | 18 | 19 | 20 | 21 |
| 22 | 23 | 24 | 25 | 26 | 27 | 28 |
| 29 | 30 | 31 |   |   |   |   |

## 1992

### January
| S | M | T | W | T | F | S |
|---|---|---|---|---|---|---|
|   |   |   | 1 | 2 | 3 | 4 |
| 5 | 6 | 7 | 8 | 9 | 10 | 11 |
| 12 | 13 | 14 | 15 | 16 | 17 | 18 |
| 19 | 20 | 21 | 22 | 23 | 24 | 25 |
| 26 | 27 | 28 | 29 | 30 | 31 |   |

### February
| S | M | T | W | T | F | S |
|---|---|---|---|---|---|---|
|   |   |   |   |   |   | 1 |
| 2 | 3 | 4 | 5 | 6 | 7 | 8 |
| 9 | 10 | 11 | 12 | 13 | 14 | 15 |
| 16 | 17 | 18 | 19 | 20 | 21 | 22 |
| 23 | 24 | 25 | 26 | 27 | 28 | 29 |

### March
| S | M | T | W | T | F | S |
|---|---|---|---|---|---|---|
| 1 | 2 | 3 | 4 | 5 | 6 | 7 |
| 8 | 9 | 10 | 11 | 12 | 13 | 14 |
| 15 | 16 | 17 | 18 | 19 | 20 | 21 |
| 22 | 23 | 24 | 25 | 26 | 27 | 28 |
| 29 | 30 | 31 |   |   |   |   |

### April
| S | M | T | W | T | F | S |
|---|---|---|---|---|---|---|
|   |   |   | 1 | 2 | 3 | 4 |
| 5 | 6 | 7 | 8 | 9 | 10 | 11 |
| 12 | 13 | 14 | 15 | 16 | 17 | 18 |
| 19 | 20 | 21 | 22 | 23 | 24 | 25 |
| 26 | 27 | 28 | 29 | 30 |   |   |

### May
| S | M | T | W | T | F | S |
|---|---|---|---|---|---|---|
|   |   |   |   |   | 1 | 2 |
| 3 | 4 | 5 | 6 | 7 | 8 | 9 |
| 10 | 11 | 12 | 13 | 14 | 15 | 16 |
| 17 | 18 | 19 | 20 | 21 | 22 | 23 |
| 24 | 25 | 26 | 27 | 28 | 29 | 30 |
| 31 |   |   |   |   |   |   |

### June
| S | M | T | W | T | F | S |
|---|---|---|---|---|---|---|
|   | 1 | 2 | 3 | 4 | 5 | 6 |
| 7 | 8 | 9 | 10 | 11 | 12 | 13 |
| 14 | 15 | 16 | 17 | 18 | 19 | 20 |
| 21 | 22 | 23 | 24 | 25 | 26 | 27 |
| 28 | 29 | 30 |   |   |   |   |

### July
| S | M | T | W | T | F | S |
|---|---|---|---|---|---|---|
|   |   |   | 1 | 2 | 3 | 4 |
| 5 | 6 | 7 | 8 | 9 | 10 | 11 |
| 12 | 13 | 14 | 15 | 16 | 17 | 18 |
| 19 | 20 | 21 | 22 | 23 | 24 | 25 |
| 26 | 27 | 28 | 29 | 30 | 31 |   |

### August
| S | M | T | W | T | F | S |
|---|---|---|---|---|---|---|
|   |   |   |   |   |   | 1 |
| 2 | 3 | 4 | 5 | 6 | 7 | 8 |
| 9 | 10 | 11 | 12 | 13 | 14 | 15 |
| 16 | 17 | 18 | 19 | 20 | 21 | 22 |
| 23 | 24 | 25 | 26 | 27 | 28 | 29 |
| 30 | 31 |   |   |   |   |   |

### September
| S | M | T | W | T | F | S |
|---|---|---|---|---|---|---|
|   |   | 1 | 2 | 3 | 4 | 5 |
| 6 | 7 | 8 | 9 | 10 | 11 | 12 |
| 13 | 14 | 15 | 16 | 17 | 18 | 19 |
| 20 | 21 | 22 | 23 | 24 | 25 | 26 |
| 27 | 28 | 29 | 30 |   |   |   |

### October
| S | M | T | W | T | F | S |
|---|---|---|---|---|---|---|
|   |   |   |   | 1 | 2 | 3 |
| 4 | 5 | 6 | 7 | 8 | 9 | 10 |
| 11 | 12 | 13 | 14 | 15 | 16 | 17 |
| 18 | 19 | 20 | 21 | 22 | 23 | 24 |
| 25 | 26 | 27 | 28 | 29 | 30 | 31 |

### November
| S | M | T | W | T | F | S |
|---|---|---|---|---|---|---|
| 1 | 2 | 3 | 4 | 5 | 6 | 7 |
| 8 | 9 | 10 | 11 | 12 | 13 | 14 |
| 15 | 16 | 17 | 18 | 19 | 20 | 21 |
| 22 | 23 | 24 | 25 | 26 | 27 | 28 |
| 29 | 30 |   |   |   |   |   |

### December
| S | M | T | W | T | F | S |
|---|---|---|---|---|---|---|
|   |   | 1 | 2 | 3 | 4 | 5 |
| 6 | 7 | 8 | 9 | 10 | 11 | 12 |
| 13 | 14 | 15 | 16 | 17 | 18 | 19 |
| 20 | 21 | 22 | 23 | 24 | 25 | 26 |
| 27 | 28 | 29 | 30 | 31 |   |   |

# 9.4 Rules of Temporal Communication

Identify three rules operating in our culture for *temporal communication* in an office of top executives at one of the conservative Fortune 500 companies. [Note: rules may be conceived of as prescriptive (indicating what should be done) or as proscriptive (indicating what should not be done).]

1.


2.


3.



Identify three rules operating in our culture for *temporal communication* in a college environment, for example, among faculty, among students, between faculty and students, etc.

1.


2.


3.



Review the six rules you have identified and respond to the following:

1. What do these rules communicate about those who adhere to them or those who enforce them?

2. Do you think these rules are cross-cultural or cross-subcultural or culture-specific? If possible, give examples of these same rules or contradictory rules operating in other cultures?

3. Do you think these rules are changing? In what direction are they changing? Why are(n't) they changing?

# Review and Discussion Questions

1. What kind of psychological time orientation did the 29-item test indicate you have? Do you think this is true? That is, are the results of the test consistent with your perception of your own time orientation? Is this time orientation productive for you, given your specific goals? If this time orientation is counterproductive, do you wish to change this? If so, how will you go about it?

2. How was your time orientation taught to you? That is, how can you account for the time orientation you now have? What kind of family and peer messages can you identify that might have played a part in the development of your time orientation?

3. Would you describe yourself as one who has primarily a displaced or a diffused time orientation? Where did you get this orientation? Are you satisfied with it? How might you go about changing it, if you wanted to?

4. Is your time orientation similar to those of your close friends? What effect does this similarity or difference in time orientation have on your relationship with your friends?

5. How might you go about using time more effectively? Indicate at least three or four areas where your use of time might be made more profitable. It may be productive to share these with members of a small group or with the entire class and construct a master list of "time management principles."

6. If you calculated your biorhythms, what comments on their usefulness or uselessness might you offer?

# Terms to Define

Chronemics

Temporal communication

Cultural time

Technical time

Formal time

Informal time

Displaced time orientation

Diffused time orientation

Psychological time

Past orientation

Present orientation

Present-moment living

Future orientation

Biological time

Biorhythm

Physical cycle

Emotional cycle

Intellectual cycle

Additional relevant terms in temporal communication

# 10

# Deception and Deception Detection

## Chapter Outline

Why Lies Fail
    *Bad Lines*
    *Emotions and Feelings*
    *Feelings about Lying*
Deception and Leakage Cues
Deception Guilt
Duping Delight
Precautions in Judging Deception

Deception and Deception Detection
  Exercises

10.1 Types of Lies
10.2 Nonverbal Cues to Lying
10.3 Nonverbal Behaviors in
     Deception
10.4 The Object in Deception
10.5 Deception Detection
10.6 Observational Record of
     Deception Communications

Review and Discussion Questions
Terms to Define

## Objectives

After completing this chapter, you should be able to:

1. explain the three major reasons why lies fail
2. define and distinguish between *deception* and *leakage cues*
3. define *deception guilt* and *duping delight*
4. explain some of the major findings concerning deception detection (see exercise 10.3)
5. identify at least five of the precautions suggested for judging deception

The area of deception and deception detection is included in nonverbal communication books because we communicate our lies and detect lies largely on the basis of nonverbal cues. It also provides a useful way of bringing together all our knowledge of nonverbal communication and applying it to a specific issue.

The research literature in deception reports numerous contradictory findings. You may find, for example, that one textbook claims that the best clue to lying is provided by the lower half of one's body while another will claim that the best clues are provided by the face and eyes. Actually, the ways in which we lie will vary tremendously depending gender, prior preparation for lying, previous successes and failures in lying successfully, the type of lie, the type of target (the person lied to), and so on.

The contradictory findings, therefore, are more apparent than real. Whereas one researcher may have focused on well-rehearsed lies, another researcher may have focused on lying without rehearsal.

> If his lips are silent he chatters with his fingertips; betrayal oozes out of him at every pore.
>
> Freud, cited in Argyle, *Bodily Communication,* p. 79

# Why Lies Fail

Nonverbal researcher Paul Ekman, in *Telling Lies: Clues to Deceit in the Marketplace, Politics, and Marriage* notes that lies fail (and hence may be detected) for at least three main reasons: bad lines, the difficulty in manipulating the expression of our feelings, and the difficulty in hiding our feelings about lying.

## Bad Lines

Perhaps the most obvious reason is that the liar uses bad lines. Such lines may be under-prepared as when the liar is confronted with questions before he or she has had adequate time to prepare the "story." But, equally revealing are lines that evidence an over-preparation. The "story" is too perfectly stated, too smooth, and so we perceive some kind of deception.

## Emotions and Feelings

A second reason is that it is extremely difficult to lie about emotions and feelings, areas on which many lies focus. It is difficult to conceal strongly felt emotions, especially when these come upon us suddenly. For example, it is difficult to conceal our sorrow immediately upon hearing of the death of a loved one. Perhaps equally difficult is portraying emotions that we do not feel. For example, it is difficult for us to pretend to be surprised when we are not. Perhaps the most difficult deception is substituting one emotion for another. For example, it is extremely difficult for us to pretend to be happy when we are really sad or to pretend to feel safe and secure when we are actually terrified.

## Feelings about Lying

The third reason lies fail concerns our feelings about lying. Our fear in being caught—which, of course, will vary with the severity of the lie and the severity of the possible punishment for getting caught—will often lead us to emit cues that tell others we are lying.

# Deception and Leakage Cues

Two kinds of cues that reveal we are lying are deception cues and leakage cues. *Deception cues* are verbal and/or nonverbal behaviors that reveal what is being said as a lie. A spouse who says, unconvincingly, "I've been working late" may signal that this is a lie by stumbling over the words, using inappropriate pauses, avoiding eye contact, and other suspect behavior.

*Leakage cues* are more revealing. Leakage cues are verbal and/or nonverbal behaviors that not only indicate that what is being said is a lie but also (unintentionally, of course) reveal what the truth is. For example, consider the spouse who is accused of carrying on an extramarital affair. The spouse denies this and in the denial makes eye contact with everyone in the room except the other person involved in the affair. This eye contact avoidance may reveal not only that an affair is going on but also with whom.

# Deception Guilt

A lie may also be discovered through cues emanating from "deception guilt." Deception guilt is guilt that we experience about lying and is distinguished from the guilt that we would feel for having commited a particular act. Thus, for example, the unfaithful spouse may not feel guilt for carrying on an extra-marital relationship but may feel guilt (deception guilt) in lying about the affair.

Of course, not all lies produce deception guilt. When, for example, we lie to protect another person, we would probably not feel guilty. Similarly, we do not regularly experience deception guilt for what are called "authorized lies." These are lies that are accepted and, in fact, built into the structure of our culture. An example of an "authorized lie" might occur when we attempt to bargain for a house we wish to buy. We might say, for example, "This is the most I will pay" when we know that we are using this low price as a bargaining device. Also, we would probably not feel deception guilt if we felt the individual asking the question has no right to the information. Thus, for example, we might have no deception guilt when we lie about our age or our sexual orientation if we feel that the person asking the question has no right to the answers.

# Duping Delight

Another give-away occurs when we reveal ourselves through "duping delight." It sometimes happens that when we are lying we experience excitement or smug satisfaction over the fact that we are lying and that we are being successful at it. Nonverbal signs of this excitement and satisfaction will often be emitted and may cue others into the fact that we are lying.

# Precautions in Judging Deception

Whenever we attempt to judge deception, to claim that someone is lying, we run considerable risk of being wrong and, as a result, incurring considerable negative reactions. Here are several suggestions or cautions to be observed in judging deception, drawn from Paul Ekman's *Telling Lies*.

---

The development of successful interpersonal relationships requires that individuals develop the ability to detect deception.

Leathers, p. 181

---

1. Make explicit to yourself the bases of your intuition. That is, bring to consciousness the reasons why you think the individual lied. This will help us identify our own mistakes and tendencies and perhaps prevent us from making them in the future. Further, this will help us to weight the evidence for or against deception more logically.

2. Recognize the two dangers inherent in judging deception:

   a. We can judge the truth a lie, or

   b. We can judge a lie the truth.

   Note that we cannot avoid both dangers. Regardless of what we do, we can make one of these two errors.

3. Not all liars leak. Not all those who lie leak cues of their deception for us to pick up and analyze. Some liars do not reveal cues of their deception. Note too that some truth-tellers may display behaviors that are often used as cues to deception. For example, if a truth-teller becomes worried about being suspected of lying, he or she may well display the heightened emotions characteristic of many liars.

4. Become aware of your own biases; we all have them. The more we learn about our own biases, the more we will be able to guard against their interfering in our judgments of deception.

5. Carefully weigh the gains and losses that may accru as a result of your detecting another's deception. For example, is it worth breaking up a close friendship because of your friend's lie.

6. Use nonverbal cues to deception only for forming hypotheses; avoid formulating conclusions on the basis of nonverbal evidence alone.

# Deception and Deception Detection Exercises

The *Workbook* exercises are designed to raise your consciousness about lying and how lies are signalled and detected through nonverbal cues. These exercises are not designed to make you a better liar or even a better lie detector. In *Types of Lies* we explore some of the major type of lies and seek to clarify what we mean by lying. In *Nonverbal Cues to Lying* we focus on deception and leakage cues, cues that "reveal" the speaker to be a liar.

*Nonverbal Behaviors and Deception* is based on an extensive review of the literature on deception. Twenty-four behaviors that have been studied as possible cues to deception are identified here and you are asked to consider the way in which you think each specific behavior would vary during lying. That is, you are asked to formulate hypotheses concerning the operation of each of these twenty-four variables in deception. Some of these behaviors are verbal behaviors. They are included here to emphasize that the verbal and the nonverbal work together in real life. It is only in academic discussions and experimental manipulations that the nonverbal component can be separated and isolated from the verbal.

In *The Object in Deception* and *Deception Detection*, classroom exercises are presented to illustrate further the operation of these various nonverbal cues. One of the purposes of these exercises is to emphasize how difficult it is to detect deception, especially when you do not know the person well and are not familiar with the general context. The *Observational Record of Deceptive Communications* should help to increase your awareness of lying and attempts to detect lying.

# 10.1   Types of Lies

Types of Lies:

Paul Ekman, in *Telling Lies: Clues to Deceit in the Marketplace, Politics, and Marriage* (New York: Norton, 1985), defines lying as "a deliberate choice to mislead a target without giving any notification of the intent to do so." Ekman also identifies a variety of types of lies. Here are several of the most popular. For each type, cite an example that you have recently witnessed or heard or read about.

1. Falsification:   the presentation of information that the liar knows to be false as if it were true.

   Example 1: "The check is in the mail."

   Example 2:

2. Misdirection:   the acknowledgement of an emotion but purposely identifying its cause incorrectly.

   Example 1: "I'm not sad about my breakup with Pat; I'm sad that you don't believe that it's really over."

   Example 2:

3. Telling the truth falsely:   the accurate reporting of the truth but in such a way as to mislead the target, perhaps by telling the truth with extreme exaggeration that it will not be believed.

   Example 1: "Oh, sure, I hate your mother; I hate your father too. And your sisters and your brother."

   Example 2:

4. Half-concealment:        the admission of only part of the truth in order to direct
                            the attention of the target away from the omitted or
                            concealed part.

                            Example 1: [in response to one's parents' question, "what
                            did you do last night?"] "We listened to music and then
                            we went for a drive." [But, saying nothing about drinking.]

                            Example 2:


5. Incorrect-inference      the telling of the truth verbally but in a way that misleads
   dodge:                   the target.

                            Example 1: [in response to a friend's asking what you think
                            of a truly horrendous outfit] "Pat! Pat! That outfit! It is really
                            something else. Where did you buy it?"

                            Example 2:

# 10.2 Nonverbal Cues to Lying

Paul Ekman, and other nonverbal researchers, identify two major types of cues to lying, behaviors that we use to evaluate the truth or falsehood of a statement. For each type of cue, identify an example that you have experienced, heard about, or read about.

Deception cue:     nonverbal (and verbal) behaviors that reveal what is said is a lie but does not reveal what is the truth.

Example 1: The unfaithful spouse who responds to questions about arriving home late with "Oh, I stopped off for a drink with some office people" may reveal (through deception cues such as awkward and frequent pauses or providing lots of irrelevant information) that this statement is a lie but does not reveal what is the actual truth.

Example 2:

Leakage cue:     nonverbal (and verbal) behaviors that reveal not only what is said is a lie but also reveals the truth.

Example 1: The unfaithful spouse who responds to questions about arriving home late with "Oh, am I late? No, nothing's the matter. I guess I just didn't notice the time" may reveal (through leakage cues such as rubbing ones lips with a handkerchief) not only that these statements are lies but that the actual reason was an act of infidelity.

Example 2:

# 10.3   Nonverbal Behaviors in Deception

The following twenty-four behaviors have all been studied as possible indicators of deception. These categories are taken from the excellent research review provided by Miron Zuckerman and Robert Driver, "Telling Lies: Verbal and Nonverbal Correlates of Deception," in Aron W. Siegman and Stanley Feldstein, eds., *Multichannel Integration of Nonverbal Behavior* (Hillsdale, New Jersey: Lawrence Erlbaum, 1985), pp. 129-147.

1. Formulate a directional hypothesis for each behavior. That is, formulate a hypothesis which states how you think the person will behave when attempting to deceive another person. The first behavior, pupil dilation, is completed to provide an example of how hypotheses may be formulated. If you think that a particular behavior would not differ during deception, state why you think this would be so.

2. Be prepared to explain why you formulated the hypothesis as you did. For example, in the pupil dilation example, you would be prepared to explain why you predicted that pupil dilation would increase (rather than decrease) during deception.

3. Note that behaviors 19-23 deal with verbal rather than nonverbal behaviors. They are included here because deception and deception detection involves both verbal and nonverbal cues.

4. What other nonverbal (or verbal) behaviors do you think might distinguish truth-telling from deception? Identify these under "additional behaviors" (items 25 to 30). Formulate hypotheses for these behaviors.


1. Pupil dilation

   Hypothesis: Pupil dilation will increase during deception.



2. Gaze

   Hypothesis:



3. Blinking

   Hypothesis:

4. Smiling

   Hypothesis:

5. Facial segmentation (the number of segments or units in the behavioral stream as identified by naive observers)

   Hypothesis:

6. Head movements

   Hypothesis:

7. Gestures or illustrators

   Hypothesis:

8. Shrugs

   Hypothesis:

9. Adaptors

   Hypothesis:

10. Foot and leg movements

    Hypothesis:

11. Postural shifts

    Hypothesis:

12. Bodily segmentation (the number of segments or units in the behavioral stream as identified by naive observers)

    Hypothesis:

13. Latency (the amount of time delay separating the ending of a question and the beginning of an answer)

    Hypothesis:

14. Response length (the number of words in responses to questions)

    Hypothesis:

15. Speech rate

    Hypothesis:

16. Speech errors

    Hypothesis:

17. Speech hesitations

    Hypothesis:

18. Pitch

    Hypothesis:

19. Negative statements

    Hypothesis:

20. Irrelevant information

    Hypothesis:

21. Self-references (for example, *I*, *me*, *my*)

    Hypothesis:

22. Immediacy (terms that indicate a relationship or a closeness between speaker and listener, for example, *us*, *we*, *our*)

    Hypothesis:

23. Leveling (also called ''allness'' terms, for example, *all*, *none*, *every*)

    Hypothesis:

24. Discrepancy (the extent to which the message communicates different emotions or feelings)

   Hypothesis:


Additional behaviors:

25.


26.


27.


28.


29.


30.

## 10.4  The Object in Deception

The objective of this exercise is to introduce some of the concepts involved in the study of nonverbal communication and deception and to identify tentatively some of the nonverbal (and verbal) behaviors that may be used as deception cues.

The procedure is relatively straightforward. Approximately five members of the class are given objects to hide on their persons without the other class members being aware of who has been given the objects or what the objects are. The class members then try to guess which students are hiding the objects.

The class members should be seated in a circle so that each member may see and communicate easily with each other member. In the first round each student in turn says "I have the object; it is. . . ." The five members who do have the object are to tell the truth while the others are to lie. The objective is for the class members to distinguish those who lied from those who told the truth by asking questions of any members they wish. Approximately 15 minutes should prove adequate for this portion of the exercise. At the end of this time, class members are to vote or otherwise indicate who they thought was telling the truth and to indicate the bases they used to draw their conclusions. Specifically, they should identify the nonverbal (and verbal) behaviors that they used as cues to their judgment of truth or deception.

# 10.5 Deception Detection*

This exercise, a modified version of the old "To Tell the Truth" television show is designed to help identify those verbal and especially those nonverbal correlates of deception. This exercise is best explained by identifying the procedures that should be followed in using it. These procedures are as follows:

1. A set of four pictures is prepared; each picture is placed in a folder.
2. Four students ("guests") are selected and are seated in front of the class. One folder is placed on each student's desk with the instructions that they are not to open the folder until the description of the photo is read to them and to the class.
3. Four panelists are next selected and are seated in front of the four "guests." The panelists and the class members are provided with a form (such as the one used here) for recording their judgments and for identifying the deception and leakage cues they perceive.
4. The instructor then reads a description of one of the pictures as the guests open their folders. This description should be true for only one of the pictures. The guest who has this picture must tell the truth; the others must lie.
5. Each of the panelists is allowed a set amount of time (2 minutes works well) to question the guests about the picture in his or her folder.
6. After each panelist has questioned the guests, each panelist votes on who he or she thinks is the truth-teller and who are the liars. Each panelist is encouraged to give specific reasons for each judgment of truth-teller or liar.
7. After all panelists have voted, the class is invited to indicate who they feel was telling the truth and who they feel was lying (and why).
8. After all votes are in, the truth-teller is instructed to stand.
9. The process is then repeated with different pictures, different guests, and different panelists. This game may be run 3 or 4 times in a normal class period.

A number of variations may be made in this basic procedure. One truth teller and three liars work well; other combinations may be tried. Further, it may prove interesting not to reveal to the panelists how many are telling the truth and how many are lying. Using all truth-tellers or all liars in one or two experiences will clearly illustrate the dangers involved and the precautions that are to be taken in making judgments of lying and truth-telling.

*The idea for this exercise was first suggested to me by Michael Hecht, Arizona State University.

## Deception and Leakage Cues

Case One:

Who tells the truth? _____

Who lies? _____

Deception and/or leakage cues: _____

_____

Case Two:

Who tells the truth? _____

Who lies? _____

Deception and/or leakage cues: _____

_____

Case Three:

Who tells the truth? _____

Who lies? _____

Deception and/or leakage cues: _____

_____

Case Four:

Who tells the truth? _____

Who lies? _____

Deception and/or leakage cues: _____

_____

## 10.6 Observational Record of Deceptive Communications

This observational record form is designed to increase your awareness of the forms and functions of deceptive communication and its role in the total communication act. For each example of deceptive communication noted, (1) describe the specific manifestation of that communication, and indicate (2) the sources and receivers of the message; (3) the specific context in which the communication occurred; (4) the message or meanings that were communicated; (5) the effects of the nonverbal communication; and (6) any additional comments or questions that you feel are relevant to understanding the specific communication.

Deception cue:


Leakage cue:


Duping delight:


Concealment:


Falsification:


Misdirection:


Incorrect inference dodge:


Tells:


Impression management behaviors:

# Review and Discussion Questions

1. Provide examples of deception and leakage cues from your own experiences, from literature, or from the media.

2. Are you an effective liar? In what situations is your effectiveness greatest? Least? Why? Are you an effective deception detector? In what situations are you most effective? Least effective? Why?

3. What nonverbal cues do you find most helpful in identifying deception in others? Are you generally correct? Generally incorrect? Explain.

4. Have you ever felt deception guilt? Explain the circumstances and the effect that this had on your subsequent behaviors.

5. Have you ever experienced duping delight? Explain the circumstances and its effect on the interaction.

6. Examine the precautions suggested for judging deception. Have you ever witnessed violations of these precautions? If so, explain the circumstances and the effects that this violation had on the subsequent behaviors of the individuals involved.

# Terms to Define

Deception

Deception cues

Leakage cues

Deception guilt

Duping delight

Lying by falsification

Lying by misdirection

Lying by telling the truth falsely

Lying by half-concealment

Lying by the incorrect-inference dodge

Additional relevant terms in deception and deception detection

# Appendix A
## Some Applications to Interpersonal Communication

241

In this appendix are included a wide variety of exercises in nonverbal communication to illustrate the wide range of applications to the general area of interpersonal communication. The purpose of this appendix is not to survey the area of interpersonal communication—there are many excellent texts that will adequately serve that purpose—but to whet your appetite for exploring some applications of nonverbal communication.

I have selected exercises that I have used in my own courses in Interpersonal Communication and in Nonverbal Communication. These exercises focus on widely different areas of interpersonal communication and are presented in no specific order.

In *Some Nonverbal Gender Differences* we provide a quiz focusing on the differences between men and women in their nonverbal behavior. These differences, it should be noted, are generally thought to be the result of learning and culture; men and women are simply taught different behaviors. There is, however, some evidence that argues that at least some of these differences have a biological base.

In *Dating Behaviors* we examine the role of nonverbal behaviors in successful and unsuccessful dating. This exercise may profitably be conducted in groups of five or six. Each group should discuss the issues and formulate recommendations. After these recommendations are formulated, each group should present the findings to the entire class. The aim of this exercise is to provide a stimulus for discussing dating behaviors and for examining, evaluating, and perhaps changing your own dating behaviors. Note that this exercise is not one in self-disclosure. It is not necessary for anyone to talk about his or her own dating experiences.

In *Nonverbal Attitudinal Communication* we examine the ways in which attitudes are communicated nonverbally. Our purpose here is to demonstrate some of the ways in which nonverbal behaviors figure in the communication of our own attitudes and in our perception of the attitudes of others.

Often interpersonal conflict gets bogged down in arguments over whether or not something was said. "You said. . . ." and "I never said. . . ." are extremely common in the world of interpersonal fighting. *Nonverbal Behaviors and Conflict Strategies* is designed to illustrate that conflict takes place nonverbally as well as verbally. We fight with our eyes, our expressions, our body movements, and our treatment of space, for example. If we are to understand conflict and improve our abilities to resolve interpersonal conflicts effectively, the role of nonverbal behaviors needs to be explored.

In *Destructive Communication Styles* we examine Virginia Satir's four communication styles that are destructive of relationships: placating, blaming, super reasonable, and irrelevant and how these styles are evidenced nonverbally. Hopefully, this exercise will sensitize us to these destructive communication styles and perhaps encourage us to examine them more closely when they appear in our own behaviors or in the behaviors of others with whom we interact.

We have probably all interacted with people who have annoying nonverbal habits. In *Dysfunctional Nonverbals* we examine these dysfunctional habits so that we may be more conscious of our own nonverbal behaviors and, if we have any of these dysfunctional habits ourselves, eliminate them.

In *Nonverbal Intercultural Communication* we examine ten intercultural situations in which there has been some kind of breakdown in communication. Examining why these breakdowns occurred may enable us to improve our own intercultural communication skills.

*Stranger in the Class* and *Who Can? Who Does? Who Knows?* are classroom "games" designed to put all your nonverbal learnings together in a given exercise. In *Stranger in the Class* you are asked to examine a person you have never seen before and make inferences about this person on the basis of his or her nonverbal behaviors. While at first you may think this is an impossible task, realize that you perform this inference-making behavior every day. We are always making inferences about others. And, of course, others are always making inferences about us. In *Who Can? Who Does? Who Knows?* you are asked to examine your fellow students (and they, you) and make inferences about them on the basis of their verbal and nonverbal behaviors. Again, this is something we have all probably been doing since this class began.

# Appendix A Exercises

After completing these exercises, you should be able to:

1. Explain some of the differences between men and women in nonverbal behavior.
2. Describe the role of nonverbal communication in successful and unsuccessful dating.
3. Describe how we communicate nonverbally when expressing a wide variety of different attitudes and in using varied conflict strategies.
4. Describe the role of nonverbal communication in the four destructive communication styles.
5. Identify and explain why a wide variety of nonverbal behaviors are dysfunctional.
6. Identify some of the nonverbal differences from one culture to another and explain how these may result in communication breakdowns between members of the different cultures.
7. Draw inferences (never conclusions) about an individual on the basis of that person's nonverbal behaviors.

# A.1  Some Nonverbal Gender Differences

The following statements summarize some of the research findings on sex differences in nonverbal communication. For each statement, insert men or *women* in each blank space. After completing all 15 statements, consider the questions for discussion.

1. _____ seem to be slightly more accurate at judging emotions from observing facial expressions than _____.

2. _____ seem better able to communicate emotions by facial expressions than _____.

3. _____ smile more than _____.

4. _____ are generally approached more closely than _____.

5. _____ reveal their emotions facially more readily than _____.

6. _____ extend their bodies, taking up greater areas of space, than _____.

7. _____ maintain more eye contect than _____ in mixed-sex dyads.

8. Both men and women, when speaking, look at _____ more than at _____.

9. In mixed-sex dyads, _____ interrupt _____ more often.

10. Some research indicates that _____ speak with greater volume than _____.

11. If a man and a woman are walking toward each other, the _____ will

    be more apt to move out of the _____'s way.

12. Unattractive _____ seem to be less accepted than are unattractive

    _____.

13. _____ both touch and are touched more than _____.

14. _____ engage in greater mutual eye contact with a same-sex partner

    than _____.

15. Same-sex pairs of _____ sit more closely together than do same-sex

    pairs of _____.


## Questions for Discussion

1. On what basis did you think that the nonverbal behavior was more accurately
   ascribed to one sex than to the other?

2. What do you think might account for the differences in nonverbal behavior?

3. Are there types of women or men in whom these differences are especially
   pronounced? Almost absent? Totally absent? On what basis do you make these
   predictions?

4. How would you go about testing one of these statements for accuracy?

5. After learning the answers given by research findings, do these seem to be consistent
   with your own observations? Note each that is not. How might you account for this
   discrepancy?

## A.2 Dating Behaviors

A young good-looking man or woman (take your pick) is fairly successful at getting first dates but second and third dates are extremely rare. The general consensus is that this person is cold, unfeeling, unemotional, and, especially, unromantic. What advice for nonverbal communication could you give this person to make him or her a more successful dating partner? What common nonverbal dating faults would you point out? Organize your advice around the following areas of nonverbal communication:

1. Advice for body communication:


2. Advice for facial and eye communication:


3. Advice for artifactual communication:


4. Advice for spatial communication:


5. Advice for tactile communication:


6. Advice for paralanguage and silence:


7. Advice for olfactic communication:


8. Advice for temporal communication:


9. Advice for deception and deception detection:

# A.3  Nonverbal Attitudinal Communication

In small groups or with the class as a whole, each member should select one of the following attitudes and identify how it is communicated nonverbally. Be as specific as possible.

Machismo


Sexism


Love


Hatred


Loneliness


Happiness


Dogmatism


Authority


High status


Sensuousness

## A.4   Nonverbal Behaviors and Conflict Strategies

Describe the nonverbal behaviors that accompany each of the following conflict strategies.

*Blaming:* accusing the other person of causing the problem or creating the conflict situation.

*Silencing:* using strategies that literally silence the other person, for example:

Crying

Force

"Heart attack"

*Gunnysacking:* storing up grievances (as in a gunnysack) and then unloading these on one's combatant.

*Minimizing:* making light of the conflict or of the other's disagreements.

*Beltlining:* hitting the other person with issues below one's level of tolerance.

*Manipulation:* avoiding open conflict and being especially charming to put the other person in a receptive and noncombative frame of mind before disagreeing.

*Nonnegotiation:* refusing to discuss the conflict or disagreement and even refusing to listen to the other person's argument or point of view.

*Emotional Appeal:* sulking, pouting, demonstrating anger, or using any means that will succeed in arousing the emotions of the other person.

*Personal Rejection:* withholding love and affection and seeking to win the argument by getting the other person to break down under this withdrawal.

*Empathic Understanding:* cooperating and understanding the other person's point of view.

# A.5   Destructive Communication Styles

In *Making Contact* Virginia Satir identifies four communication styles that are destructive of relationships:

*Placating:* tries to please everyone at all times in order to retain their love; often makes others feel guilt or pity

*Blaming:* tries to force people into obeying; blames others for everything, amkes others feel fearful and helpless

*Super reasonable:* emphasizes logic and ideas to demonstrate how smart he or she is, expresses no feelings; makes others feel inferior and stupid

*Irrelevant:* secures attention through any means available; makes others feel off balance

With this as a background, small groups are formed. The small group is given a problem to solve and each member is given one of the above communication styles to role-play while attempting to solve the problem. Approximately 15 minutes should be given to the problem solving discussion with individual members playing their assigned roles. Each group should be assigned two observers who will observe and record the nonverbal behaviors of the members. An observation form suitable for this purpose is provided below. After all observations have been recorded, members should direct their attention to the analysis of the observation forms and to the following questions:

1. Do the different communication styles have nonverbal correlates? That is, can we identify specific nonverbal behaviors that are common to each of these four destructive communication styles?

2. What effect do these nonverbal behaviors have on the group members? That is, how do members feel about these nonverbal behaviors? How are they responded to?

3. Can types of interactions be identified in which these nonverbals are most likely to occur?

4. Can you identify people you know who frequently communicate in one of these four styles? Do they also evidence any consistent nonverbal patterns? What other nonverbal behaviors might logically accompany these communication styles?

## Observation Form

**Instructions:** Observe the group members and record any nonverbal behaviors that communicate the placating, blaming, super reasonable, or irrelevant communication styles. Pay particular attention to nonverbal cues of body posture, body orientation, body movements, facial expressions, eye movements, eye contact, physical closeness, paralanguage (rate, volume, rhythm, pitch, hesitations, prolonged silences), and touching.

Placating behaviors:

---

Blaming behaviors:

---

Super reasonable behaviors:

---

Irrelevant behaviors:

# A.6  Dysfunctional Nonverbals

Each person in the class or in the small group should record at least three nonverbal behaviors that he or she feels are dysfunctional.

A nonverbal behavior may be considered dysfunctional if it:

1. interferes with the message being received as the sender wishes;
2. creates interactional or relational difficulties for the individuals;
3. makes one or more persons psychologically uncomfortable;
4. contributes to negative impressions of one or more individuals;
5. contributes to member dissatisfaction with the communication interaction; or
6. contributes to communication inefficiency.

A composite list is made up and distributed to all members or compiled on the chalkboard. Members of the group or class should analyze these nonverbals, covering at least the following issues:

1. Why are these nonverbals dysfunctional?
2. What impressions of the sender do we get on the basis of these nonverbals? That is, how do they influence our perception of who this person is and what this person is like?
3. How can we eliminate/control these behaviors?
4. Where and when are these dysfunctional behaviors most likely to occur?
5. What other communication behaviors accompany these dysfunctional ones?
6. Are any of these dysfunctional behaviors more common to one sex than to the other? Why? What consequences do these behaviors have for sex stereotyping? For female-female interaction? For male-male interaction? For female-male interaction?

# A.7 Nonverbal Intercultural Communication*

This exercise is designed to raise some of the reasons for ineffective intercultural communication and to sensitize you to at least some of the many communication differences between and among cultures.

For each of the following situations, identify at least one possible reason for the failure to communicate effectively.

1. An American invites a Filopino co-worker to dinner. The Filopino politely refuses. The American is hurt and feels that the Filopino does not want to be friendly. The Filopino is hurt and concludes that the invitation was not extended sincerely.

2. A young American girl is talking with an older Indonesian man. She communicates as if she were talking with an American man. After a brief interchange, the Indonesian leaves thinking the girl was disrespectful.

3. An American and an Arab are talking in an open yard. After a brief discussion the American concludes that the Arab was pushy and overly familiar; the Arab concludes that the American was cold and "standoffish."

4. An American and a Moslem are having dinner. The American, being left handed, eats and drinks with his left hand. When another dinner is proposed the Moslem refuses; the American, the Moslem thinks, is obscene.

5. An American and a Latin American are having dinner in a Latin American restaurant. The American raises his hand and tries to catch the waiter's eye but to no avail. The Latin American hits the water glass with the fork. The waiter comes to take the order. The Latin American concludes that the American is shy and lacks assertiveness. The American concludes that the Latin American is rude and overly aggressive.

6. An American couple living in Europe invites another couple (co-workers) to dinner at their home. All goes well. Several weeks later the European couple invites the American couple to dinner but at a local restaurant. The American couple feels somewhat insulted and concludes that the European couple did not wish to share the intimacy of their home and that they therefore did not really want to become friends.

7. An American teacher gives a lecture in Beijing, China to a group of Chinese college students. The students listen politely but make no comments and ask no questions. The American teacher concludes that her lecture was uninteresting. Her colleague consoles her by saying that the students didn't understand her lecture and suggests that on future occasions she attempt to simplify some of the more complex material.

8. A college student just hears the news that her favorite uncle has died. She bites her lip, pulls herself up, and politely excuses herself from the group of foreign students with whom she was having dinner. The Russian thinks: "How unfriendly." The Italian thinks: "How insincere." The Brazilian thinks: "How unconcerned." The fellow American thinks: "How brave."

9. The Arab college student leaves the windows of his dormitory room open and blasts his stereo. The American students overhearing the stereo cannot understand how this normally polite and considerate student should suddenly act so inconsiderately.

10. A politician is scheduled to give a 20-minute speech on economic trends. He speaks for exactly 20 minutes. The American listeners conclude that the speaker had prepared well and was considerate of his audience. The Latin American listeners conclude that the speaker was not really interested in his topic or his audience.

*Many of these examples were drawn from J. Vernon Jensen's excellent "Perspective on Nonverbal Intercultural Communication," in *Intercultural Communication: A Reader*, 4th ed., eds. Larry A. Samovar and Richard E. Porter (Belmont, Calif.: Wadsworth, 1985), pp. 256-272.

# A.8 Stranger in the Class*

The purpose of this exercise is to explore the bases you use in perceiving and judging people you see for the first time. Since we all make judgments of people on seeing them, we need to investigate the ways and means we use in making these judgments.

A stranger (someone you have not seen before) will be brought into the class. Look the stranger over and answer the questions below. For this phase of the exercise, no interaction between you and the stranger should take place. Use the number "1" to mark your answers.

After answering all the questions you will be able to interact with the stranger for 5 or 10 minutes. Ask him or her any questions you wish, though none can be directly related to the questions asked below. The stranger should answer any questions posed as fully as he or she thinks necessary. The stranger should not, however, answer any questions that relate directly to the questions posed on the following pages. After this interaction, again answer the questions, this time using "2" to mark your answers.

After these answers have been recorded, the stranger or the instructor will go over each of the questions, specifying which answers the stranger thinks are most appropriate.

The stranger would most likely:

1. read

_____ a comedy

_____ a classic Russian novel

_____ a sex-improvement manual

_____ a philosophical essay

_____ a current popular novel

_____ a Gothic romance

2. see

_____ a mystery movie

_____ a romantic movie

_____ a western

_____ a comedy

_____ an erotic movie

_____ a foreign film

3. participate in

_____ baseball

_____ tennis

_____ golf

_____ skiing

_____ none of these

4. listen to

_____ classical music

_____ rock music

_____ country and western

_____ popular music

_____ disco

255

5. watch on television
   _____ a situation comedy
   _____ the news
   _____ an educational show
   _____ a detective show
   _____ a sports show
   _____ a soap opera

6. prefer to be
   _____ alone
   _____ in a crowd
   _____ with one person

7. go to
   _____ a rock concert
   _____ an art museum
   _____ a baseball game
   _____ an opera
   _____ a play
   _____ a movie

8. look for in a mate
   _____ intelligence
   _____ looks
   _____ personality
   _____ money

9. subscribe to
   _____ *Playboy/Playgirl*
   _____ *National Geographic*
   _____ *Time/Newsweek*
   _____ *Popular Mechanics*
   _____ *Modern Bride*

10. behave
    _____ as an extrovert
    _____ an an introvert
    _____ an an ambivert

11. act
    _____ aggressively
    _____ assertively
    _____ nonassertively

12. be
    _____ very energetic
    _____ very lazy
    _____ fairly energetic
    _____ fairly lazy

13. behave in most situations
    _____ very emotionally
    _____ very rationally
    _____ fairly emotionally
    _____ fairly rationally

14. What is the stranger's
    Age _____
    Occupation _____
    Educational level reached _____
    Relational status _____
    Financial status _____

Describe the stranger's personality in two, three, or four adjectives. How does the stranger feel now? Explain.

Discussion should focus on at least the following:

1. What cues (verbal and nonverbal) were most significant in revealing what the stranger was like?

2. Has your implicit personality theory enabled you to make inferences about the stranger's personality or behaviors? Explain.

3. Did primacy-recency influence your impressions? Did, for example, your first impressions serve as a kind of filter through which you examined and evaluated further and later information?

4. Did members of the class respond very differently to this stranger? To what can you attribute these different perceptions? For example, did the male and female students see the stranger differently?

5. Did the self-fulfilling prophecy operate here in any way? Did stereotyping? How?

*This exercise, though in a somewhat different form, was suggested by James C. McCroskey, Carl E. Larson, and Mark L. Knapp in their *Teacher's Manual for An Introduction to Interpersonal Communication* (Englewood Cliffs, N.J.: Prentice-Hall, 1971).

# A.9 Who Can? Who Does? Who Knows?

The purpose of this exercise is to explore some of the verbal and nonverbal cues that people give off and that others receive and use in formulating assumptions about the knowledge, ability, and personality of another. The exercise should serve as a useful summary of the concepts and principles of verbal and nonverbal communication and of perception.

The entire class should form a circle so that each member may see each other member without straining. If members do not know all the names of their classmates, some system of name tags should be used for this exercise.

Each student should examine the following list of phrases and should write the name of one student to whom he or she feels each statement applies in the column labeled "Who?" Be certain to respond to all statements. Although one name may be used more than once, the exercise will prove more effective if a wide variety of names are chosen. Unless the class is very small, no name should be used more than 4 times.

Next to each student's name, record a *certainty rating* in the column labeled "CR," indicating how sure you are of your choices. Use a 5-point scale with 5 indicating great certainty and 1 indicating great uncertainty.

After the names and certainty ratings have been written down for *each* statement by *each* student, the following procedure may prove useful. The instructor or group leader selects a statement and asks someone specifically, or the class generally, what names were written down. (There is no need to tackle the statements in the order they are given here.) Before the person whose name was put down is asked if the phrase is correctly or incorrectly attributed to him or her, some or all of the following questions should be considered.

1. Why did you select the name you did? What was there about this person that led you to think that this phrase applied to him or her? What *specific* verbal or nonverbal cues led you to your conclusion?

2. What additional verbal and/or nonverbal cues would you need to raise your degree of certainty?

3. Is your response at all a function of a stereotype you might have of this individual's ethnic, religious, racial, or sexual identification? For example, how many women's names were put down for the questions or phrases about the saws or pistons? How many men's names were put down for the statements pertaining to cooking or using a sewing machine?

4. Did anyone give off contradictory cues such that some cues were appropriate for a specific phrase and others were not appropriate? Explain the nature of these contradictory cues.

5. How pleased or disappointed are the people whose names have been proposed? Why? Where there any surprises? Why were some of these guesses unexpected?

6. How do you communicate your ''self'' to others? How do you communicate what you know, think, feel, and do to your peers?

**Who?**    **CR**

_____  _____  1. goes to the professional theater a few times a year

_____  _____  2. has taken a vacation outside the country in the last 12 months

_____  _____  3. likes to cook

_____  _____  4. watches soap operas on a fairly regular basis

_____  _____  5. wants lots of children

_____  _____  6. knows the function of a car's pistons

_____  _____  7. knows how to knit

_____  _____  8. would vote against the ERA

_____  _____  9. has a pet

_____  _____  10. has seen a pornographic (XXX rated) movie within the last 3 months

_____  _____  11. knows how to wire a lamp

_____  _____  12. has been to an opera

_____  _____  13. is a member of an organized sports team

_____  _____  14. watches television for an average of at least 3 hours per day

_____  _____  15. knows who played Superman in the television series

_____  _____  16. has cried over a movie in the last few months

_____  _____  17. fluently speaks a foreign language

_____  _____  18. is married

_____  _____  19. has many close friends

_____  _____  20. knows how potatoes should be planted

_____  _____  21. knows who Edward R. Murrow was

_____ _____ 22. knows the differences among a hacksaw, a jigsaw, and a copingsaw

_____ _____ 23. knows the ingredients for a bloody Mary

_____ _____ 24. knows how to make a hollandaise sauce

_____ _____ 25. knows the function of the spleen

_____ _____ 26. knows what an armoire is

_____ _____ 27. can name all 12 signs of the zodiac

_____ _____ 28. has a car in his or her immediate family costing over $20,000

_____ _____ 29. would come to the aid of a friend even at great personal sacrifice

_____ _____ 30. is frequently infatuated (or in love)

_____ _____ 31. would like, perhaps secretly, to be a movie star

_____ _____ 32. knows how to play bridge

_____ _____ 33. enjoys reading poetry

_____ _____ 34. knows where Liechtenstein is

_____ _____ 35. knows the legal status of Puerto Rico

_____ _____ 36. keeps a diary or a journal

_____ _____ 37. knows how many members are on a soccer team

_____ _____ 38. knows what SALT stands for

_____ _____ 39. knows who the heavyweight boxing champion is

_____ _____ 40. knows what the prime rate means

_____ _____ 41. was a member of the Boy Scouts or Girl Scouts

_____ _____ 42. is very religious

_____ _____ 43. would describe himself or herself as a political activist

_____ _____ 44. wants to go to graduate, law, or medical school

_____ _____ 45. would vote in favor of gay rights legislation

_____ _____ 46. is planning to get married within the next 12 months

_____ _____ 47. is going to make a significant contribution to society

_____ _____ 48. is going to be a millionaire

_____ _____ 49. is a real romantic

_____ _____ 50. would emerge as a leader in a small group situation

# Review and Discussion Questions

1. In what ways do gender differences in nonverbal communication create difficulties for opposite-sex interaction? Can you cite examples in which nonverbal behaviors are misinterpreted because men and women have different meanings for the same behaviors?

2. What nonverbals seem to characterize effective date-asking behavior? Put differently, how would you describe the nonverbal behaviors of the effective date-asker?

3. What attitudes do you think your nonverbal behaviors communicate about you? Are you satisfied? Dissatisfied? If you are dissatisfied, how would you go about changing this situation?

4. Describe your own nonverbal behaviors during an interpersonal conflict situation. Describe the nonverbal behaviors of the members of your family during interpersonal conflict? What behaviors seem effective in resolving the conflict and in helping the relationship get back on an even keel? What behaviors seem ineffective and seem to contribute to prolonging the conflict, delaying a resolution, and in hurting the relationship?

5. In Exercise A.5 (*Destructive Communication Styles*) we examined the nonverbal behaviors of destructive communication. How would you describe constructive communication? Can you identify styles of constructive communication? What nonverbal behaviors would characterize each style?

6. Can you identify any dysfunctional nonverbals in your own communication behaviors? If you can, what are you going to do about them? How?

7. Can you provide any personal examples of miscommunication due to different meanings being attributed to behaviors by different cultures?

8. If you were the stranger in the class (that is, if you met the class for the first time) what do you think the class members would have said about you on each of the questions posed in Exercise A.8 (Stranger in the Class)? What specific nonverbals contributed most to these impressions? Do you have any nonverbals that mislead people into assuming you are what you are not?

9. Review the list of items provided in Exercise A.9 (*Who Can? Who Does? Who Knows?*) and indicate the single most important nonverbal behavior for each item. That is, start with the first item and identify the single nonverbal behavior that would be most revealing in determining if a specific person "goes to the professional theatre a few times a year" and so on down the list.

10. Design an exercise in nonverbal communication similar to those included in this workbook that will illustrate the role of nonverbal communication in some aspect of interpersonal relationships.

# Terms to Define

Nonverbal gender differences

Nonverbal conflict strategies

Destructive communication styles

Nonverbal placating behaviors

Nonverbal blaming behaviors

Nonverbal super reasonable behaviors

Nonverbal irrelevant behaviors

Dysfunctional nonverbals

Nonverbal intercultural communication

Additional relevant terms in nonverbal interpersonal communication

# Appendix B
## Researching Nonverbal Communication

### Appendix Outline

This appendix contains five exercises designed to introduce you to research in nonverbal communication. Up until now, you have functioned primarily as consumers of research conducted by others. Now, it's your turn to become researchers and to discover something about nonverbal communication. Of course, the research that enters the professional journals is much more detailed, more carefully controlled, and more thoroughly analyzed than the research suggested here. These exercises, however, will accomplish a great deal. Among the most important goals are that you will learn how research is conducted by actually going through the process from the formulation of a research question to the actual drawing of conclusions on the basis of your observations. In going through this process you will learn a variety of skills such as how to ask answerable questions, how to operationally define variables, how to record data, how to search the scholarly literature in an area, and numerous other skills to be identified throughout the exercises. You will also, I think, gain a greater appreciation for the research findings that appear in your textbooks generally.

The first exercise, *Abstracting a Research Study*, provides you with an opportunity to dissect a previously published research study so that you will see more clearly each of the several steps to be taken in conducting your own research. In *Formulating Hypotheses* we consider perhaps the most important aspect of research, that of asking questions and phrasing these as testable hypotheses.

In *Defining Nonverbal Variables Operationally* you will gain experience in defining nonverbal communication variables in *measurable* terms. *Evaluating "Research" Claims* should prove both informative and entertaining. This exercise asks that you evaluate "research headlines" from a variety of nonverbal communication areas. The exercise should sensitize you to the difficulties involved in drawing conclusions about nonverbal behaviors.

The last exercise—usually a standard project in courses in nonverbal communication—*Designing and Conducting a Research Project in Nonverbal Communication*, takes you through the entire research process—from the formulating of a question to the presentation of your findings to an audience.

# Appendix B Exercises

After completing these exercises, you should be able to:

1. abstract a research study
2. formulate testable hypotheses from general questions
3. distinguish between null and directional hypotheses and phrase correctly both types
4. operationally define a variety of nonverbal variables
5. research a topic in the scholarly literature
6. design a quantitative study to test a hypothesis
7. present the findings of a research study to an audience

# B.1  Abstracting a Research Study

Excellent training in understanding and in conducting research is provided by practice in abstracting research studies. For this exercise, each student is asked to abstract one article from those listed in the bibliography under "articles." Unless instructed otherwise, write your abstract according to the following directions.

Your abstract should be one-page in length, single spaced. [This one-page restriction will simplify the process of distributing copies to members of the class, should that prove desirable. With this distribution procedure, one or more classes may be effectively devoted to the discussion, analysis, and critique of a wide variety of research studies. The abstract is also restricted to one-page to emphasize the need to identify the essentials of a research study and not get lost in any peripheral issues.]

At the top of the page provide the bibliographic reference as it appears in the bibliography in this workbook. The remaining page space should be devoted to the following divisions. Identify them in your report as they are identified here.

*Background and Purpose(s).* State the general purpose(s) of the study and any essential background material that may be provided. If this study contains specific hypotheses that are tested (as most will), identify these in this section.

*Methods and Procedures.* Describe the way in which the study was carried out. For example, identify the subjects used, the tests given or measurements taken, and any other considerations that figure into the general design of the research that seem relevant.

*Findings/Results.* Identify what the researcher discovered. If hypotheses were involved in this study, identify whether or not they were rejected.

*Conclusions.* What conclusions did the researcher draw on the basis of the study's findings? [In some studies the conclusions are almost identical with the "findings." In other studies they may be very different.]

If these abstracts are to be discussed in class, be prepared (1) to present a brief three to five minute summary of the research study and (2) to present a brief evaluation of the study.

# B.2  Formulating Hypotheses

Presented below are questions about various aspects of nonverbal communication. In order to familiarize yourself with some of the essential preliminaries to conducting research in nonverbal communication:

A. Phrase each question as a null hypothesis, that is, as a statement that asserts no differences exist. For example, *there is no difference between men and women in the amount of space they take up when seated in a public place.*

B. Define all terms that require definition as appropriate. Define all nonverbal variables operationally, that is, in terms of how they would be measured. Specify the informants and/or subjects you would use, their number, sex, age, nationality, status, or any other characteristic that might have some bearing on the behavior under investigation.

C. Design a study that would enable you to test your hypothesis.


Questions for Conversion to Hypotheses

1. Are there gender differences in body satisfaction?

2. Do women and men prefer the same colors in clothing?

3. Are young and old touched to the same degree and in the same places?

4. Do successful and unsuccessful college students view time in the same way?

5. Do men and women respond in the same way to territorial invasion?

6. Do popular and unpopular college students engage in different eye behavior?

7. Do different age groups use silence in the same way or to serve the same functions?

8. Is one age group better at deception or at deception detection than are others?

# B.3   Defining Nonverbal Variables Operationally

This exercise is designed to provide some experience in operationally defining your variables for your research project in nonverbal communication. It should also provide additional practice in hypothesis formulation.

When we define a variable operationally, we define it in terms of the operations that are necessary to observe that variable. For example, Edward Hall defines the four interpersonal distances operationally as follows: intimate distance = touching to 18 inches; personal distance = 1.5 to 4 feet; social distance = 4 to 12 feet; and public distance = 12 feet to more than 25 feet. Notice that we can observe any interaction and easily observe intimate, personal, social, or public distances according to the definitions given by Hall. We might, for example, operationally define the tendency to avoid touching as the score that a person would make on the Touch Avoidance Scale presented in Chapter 6.

For each of the statements presented below: (1) phrase each one as a testable hypothesis and (2) operationally define each of the nonverbal variables and their accompanying adjective italicized below.

1. As anxiety increases so does the *frequency of self-adaptors*.

2. Women (men) are more effective *facial managers* than are men (women).

3. People who dislike each other avoid *direct eye contact* with each other.

4. Middle income people wear *more jewelry* than do either low income or high income people.

5. Women (men) maintain a more *comfortable face-to-face speaking distance* than do men (women).

6. Happy people *more frequently initiate touching* than do unhappy people.

7. People who are more educated have *more fluent speech* than less educated people.

8. Men and women do not have the same *smell preferences*.

9. Success in college can be reliably estimated from a student's *time orientation*.

10. People in same-sex dyads are better able to *detect lying* in each other than are people in opposite-sex dyads.

# B.4  Evaluating "Research" Claims

The purpose of this exercise is to stimulate some initial exploration of research in nonverbal communication and to raise pertinent questions concerning research claims and their evaluation. This exercise should also sensitize you to the gap that exists between claims in the popular press and the research evidence necessary to substantiate these claims.

Presented below are "headlines" that might appear in a magazine or newspaper. Like real headlines, those presented here make some fairly powerful claims. Read over the headlines and for each (1) identify the hypothesis(es) that would have to be tested to make the claim(s) as presented in the headline and (2) identify and briefly outline the kind of research study and research findings that would be necessary to substantiate the claims made in the headlines.

1. *When in doubt, dismiss the verbal, believe the nonverbal.*

   Researchers at the Institute for Behavioral Studies in Nonverbal Communication report that people reveal their true feelings nonverbally. When the verbal and the nonverbal messages contradict each other, researchers say, believe the nonverbal. In these situations, the nonverbal messages reveal the truth.

2. *Scientists discover the key to attraction: mirroring.*

   Researchers at the University of Nonverbal Communication report that when one person imitates (or mirrors) the behavior of another, it means that he or she is attracted to that person.

3. *Your facial expression reveals your personality!*

   Scientists discover eight facial expressions are keys to understanding your personality.

4. *Nonverbal researchers find color preferences reveal the inner you.*

   Your own color preferences can reveal your ambition or depression, whether you are an extrovert or an introvert, and how quick you are to judge people. It even reveals your degree of sexual satisfaction.

5. *Want ot exert your power? Want to overpower your colleagues? The secret, scientists discover, is to do business in your primary territory.*

   Researchers at the Institute for Advanced Study in Human Communication have discovered that people can exercise their power best when they are in their primary territory.

6. *Mothers train their sons to be insensitive.*

   Tactile communication researchers at the College of Nonverbal Study report that the lack of sensitivity shown in many men, originates in infancy when mothers avoid touching their sons.

7. *Want to be believed? Talk fast.*

   Communicologists have recently discovered what advertisers have long known: speakers are believed more when they talk fast.

8. *Use smell to ensure compatibility.*

   Recently, olfactory researchers have discovered that the smell of a potential relational partner can be used to determine compatibility. People with "compatable smells" stand a greater chance of establishing a lasting relationship than do those without compatable smells, researchers report.

9. *Increase your income by focusing on the future.*

   Chronemic researchers at the International Society for the Study of Nonverbal Communication report that persons who are oriented to the future will earn significantly more income than will those who are oriented to the past or the present.

10. *You can learn to lie more effectively.*

    Researchers studying deception and especially deception and leakage cues—those signals that people give off that reveal they are lying—report that we can increase our effectiveness in lying by simple rehearsal.

# B.5 Designing and Conducting a Research Project in Nonverbal Communication

*Purpose:* This research project in nonverbal communication has two major purposes. The first is to provide you with an opportunity to investigate in depth an area of nonverbal communciation that is of special interest to you. The second is to familiarize you with some of the basic procedures that are followed in conducting research, including the formulation of a hypothesis, the design of the study, the collection of relevant data, the analysis of that data, and the presentation of the methods, procedures, and results of the study to the academic community and the public at large.

*Step One. Formulate a Hypothesis.*

For purposes of this project, all hypotheses should focus on one or more aspects of nonverbal communication and its (their) relationship to one of the following variables: gender, age, nationality, socioeconomic status, or relational status. Select your hypothesis from an area of nonverbal communication that is especially interesting to you. Select a nonverbal variable for which there is some reason for expecting or hypothesizing a difference on the basis of gender, age, nationality, socioeconomic status, or relational status. [Note: Hypotheses for this exercise are restricted to these five variables to simplify this experience for an introductory course. Normally, of course, research hypotheses are drawn from implications from theory and from directions for research suggested by other research findings.]

The Null Hypothesis

For this project it will probably be best to formulate a null hypothesis, that is, a hypothesis that claims there is no difference between the sexes, between different age groups, and so on. For example:

> There is no difference between men and women in color preferences.

> There is no difference between young men and old men in their response to touch violations.

> There is no difference between happily married and unhappily married couples in their eye contact behavior.

The Directional Hypothesis

A directional hypothesis is a hypothesis that states the direction of the differences you predict will be found. For example, hypotheses dealing with the issues identified to illustrate the null hypothesis above, might be phrased as directional hypotheses as follows:

Women will prefer a wider variety of colors than men or women will prefer brighter colors than men

Young men will respond less negatively than older men to touch violations

Happily married couples will look into each other's eyes more frequently and will maintain the eye contact for longer periods of time than will unhappily married couples

Note that in the last hypothesis, we really have two separate hypotheses: (1) happily married couples will engage in mutual eye contact more often and (2) happily married couples will maintain this mutual eye contact for longer periods of time.

*Step Two. Research this Area.*

Research this area in at least two ways. First, read in textbooks or other general sources about the general area of nonverbal communication on which you are focusing. Suitable sources for this research phase are provided in this workbook and in your textbook. Second, read the relevant research studies reported in the journals. Begin with those studies cited in the various textbooks and then explore additional and more recent studies cited in, for example, *Psychological Abstracts, Sociological Abstracts, Communication Abstracts,* and other abstracts and indexes.

*Step Three. Design Your Study.*

In designing this study, follow these basic steps.

1. Operationally define all relevant terms. Included in these operational definitions will be appropriate means of isolating and measuring the relevant variables. Thus, for example, *touch* might be operationally defined as the number of times one person's body makes contact with another person's body during a five-minute interaction. *Relational status* might be operationally defined in terms of the categories you would use to classify the various possibilities. One such system might be: (1) single/never married; (2) in a primary relationship but not married; (3) married; (4) divorced; and (5) widowed.

2. Select appropriate means for observing the operation of the variables, including, for example, the subjects or informants you will use, the recording instruments, the responses to be observed, the way in which the responses or observations will be recorded.

### Step Four. Conduct Your Study.

Follow through. For example, observe your subjects, question your informants, record the relevant responses.

### Step Five. Analyze Your Data.

After all the data have been collected, analyze them. If you know statistics, apply the appropriate statistical tests. If you do not know statistics at this time, use simple averages, percentages, or any other type of summary statistic that is appropriate. Represent these data visually in a bar graph, pie chart, or in some other appropriate visual form.

### Step Six. Formulate Your Conclusions.

After you have analyzed the data, refer back to your hypothesis and see if there is sufficient evidence to enable you to reject it if it is a null hypothesis or accept it if it is a directional hypothesis. That is, on the basis of the data you have collected, make a judgment about the validity of your hypothesis. Also, provide some explanation as to why you have found what you have found. In discussing the results and conclusions be certain to integrate previous research findings and show clearly where your results fit into what we already know about nonverbal communication.

### Step Seven. Write Up the Study.

Follow the format suggested below in writing up your study unless other directions are given.

[Title]: Give your study a title—a short but relevant name. Under this title, include your name.

*Abstract:* Summarize the purpose, design, and major findings of your study in 100 words or less.

*Background and Hypotheses:* Here state the general nature of the area you will investigate and its significance to communication and to human behavior generally. Next, and most important, state your hypothesis and the reasons for its formulation. Most appropriate are reasons derived from well-ground theory and previous empirical research.

*Methods and Procedures:* Here briefly but completely state the methods and procedures you used to investigate this hypothesis.

*Findings/Results:* Here present your results (in numerical form and in some kind of table or chart) and discuss these results, including how you analyzed the data.

*Conclusions:* Here discuss what these data tell us about nonverbal communication and what conclusions your findings suggest about nonverbal communication. Relate these results and conclusions directly to your hypothesis.

*References:* Append a list of all those references that are directly relevant to your study *and* that you have used *and* referred to in your paper. Do not list sources that you have consulted but not used in the actual paper. Use the APA Style Manual for writing up the paper and for bibliographic reference.

In addition to this written presentation, be prepared to discuss this research project with the class in a brief, informal interaction of approximately five minutes.

# Review and Discussion Questions

1. One view of research would hold that we do research every day when, for example, we examine specific instances of a category and then conclude something about the category as a whole. Examine your attitudes toward the following categories and try to discover how you developed these attitudes (for example, expressed belief of family members, taught in school, heard on a particular situation comedy show, saw in an advertisement):

    a. extremely beautiful women and extremely handsome men

    b. people with very thick glasses

    c. people who wear extremely tight fitting clothes

    d. men with high voices

    e. an extremely attractive person romantically involved with an extremely unattractive person

2. Can you think of a question about nonverbal communication that is not, by its very nature, amenable to scientific investigation?

3. How would you go about researching your own nonverbal effectiveness-ineffectiveness? Design a brief study that would help you to gain this insight.

4. Examine a specific research study that is discussed in your textbook or in this workbook. That is, read the original study as it was published in a scholarly journal. Did the textbook author(s) report the research accurately? Was the research study used in the textbook effectively? Were the limitations of the study noted in the textbook? What else might the textbook author(s) have said about this research study?

# Terms to Define

Research abstract

Hypothesis

Null hypothesis

Directional hypothesis

Operational definition

Research design

Additional relevant terms in nonverbal communication research

# Helpful Readings in Nonverbal Communication Research

Anderson, James A. *Communication Research: Issues and Methods.* New York: McGraw-Hill, 1987.

Bowers, John W. and John A. Courtright. *Communication Research Methods.* Glenview, Illinois: Scott, Foresman, 1984.

Emmert, Philip and Larry L. Barker. *Measurement of Communication Behavior.* New York: Longman, 1989.

Emmert, Philip and William D. Brooks, eds. *Methods of Research in Communication.* Boston: Houghton Mifflin, 1970.

Gudykunst, William and Y. Y. Kim, eds. *Methods for Intercultural Communication Research.* Beverly Hills, California: Sage, 1984.

Leathers, Dale G. *Orientations to Researching Communication.* Chicago, Ill.: Science Research Associates, 1978.

Rubin, Rebecca B., Alan M. Rubin, and Linda Piele. *Communication Research: Strategies and Sources.* Belmont, California: Wadsworth, 1986.

Tucker, Raymond K., R. L. Weaver, and C. Berryman-Fink. *Research in Speech Communication.* Englewood Cliffs, New Jersey: Prentice-Hall, 1981.

Smith, Mary John. *Contemporary Communication Research Methods.* Belmont, Calif.: Wadsworth, 1988.

Williams, Frederick. *Reasoning with Statistics: How to Read Quantitative Statistics,* 3rd ed. New York: Holt, 1986.

# Readings in Nonverbal Communication

The following bibliography in nonverbal communication, although relatively long, represents just a small part of the research and theory in nonverbal communication. The books and articles listed here should provide a useful reference list for both introductory and intermediate study in nonverbal communication.

In order to keep abreast of the current literature and for more advanced study, examine current issues of *Journal of Nonverbal Behavior, Communication Monographs, Human Communication Research*, and various other journals in communication, psychology, sociology, and related areas.

# Books

Altman, I. *The Environment and Social Behavior.* Belmont, California: Wadsworth, 1975.

Argyle, Michael. *Bodily Communication*, 2nd ed. New York: New York: Methuen & Co. Ltd., 1988.

Audrey, Robert. *The Territorial Imperative.* New York: Atheneum, 1966.

Benson, Thomas W. and Kenneth D. Frandsen. *An Orientation to Nonverbal Communication.* Chicago, Illinois: Science Research Associates, 1976.

Birdwhistell, Ray L. *Kinesics and Context: Essays on Body Motion Communication.* Philadelphia: University of Pennsylvania Press, 1970.

Birren, Faber. *Color: A Survey in Words and Pictures.* Secaucus, New Jersey: Citadel Press, 1963.

Bosmajian, Haig A., ed. *The Rhetoric of Nonverbal Communication.* Glenview, Illinois: Scott, Foresman, 1971.

Buck, Ross. *The Communication of Emotion.* New York: Guilford Press, 1984.

Burgoon, Judee and Thomas Saine. *The Unspoken Dialogue: An Introduction to Nonverbal Communication.* Boston, Massachusetts: Houghton Mifflin, 1978.

Clark, Linda. *The Ancient Art of Color Therapy.* New York: Pocket Books, 1975.

Colton, Helen. *Touch Therapy.* New York: Zebra, 1983.

Cottle, T. J. *Perceiving Time: A Psychological Investigation with Men and Women.* New York: Wiley, 1976.

Critchley, Macdonald. *The Language of Gesture.* London: Arnold, 1939.

Darwin, Charles. *The Expression of the Emotions in Man and Animals* [1972]. New York: Philosophical Library, 1955.

Davis, Flora. *Inside Intuition: What We Know About Nonverbal Communication.* New York: McGraw-Hill, 1973.

Davis, Martha. *Understanding Body Movement: An Annotated Bibliography.* New York: Arno Press, 1972.

Davitz, Joel R., ed. *The Communication of Emotional Meaning.* New York: McGraw-Hill, 1964.

DeVito, Joseph A. and Michael L. Hecht, eds. *The Nonverbal Communication Reader.* Prospect Heights, Illinois: Waveland Press, 1990.

Donaghy, William C. *Our Silent Language: An Introduction to Nonverbal Communication.* Dubuque, Iowa: Gorsuch Scarisbrick, 1980.

Dreyfuss, Henry. *Symbol Sourcebook*. New York: McGraw-Hill, 1971.

Efron, David. *Gesture, Race and Culture*. The Hague: Mouton, 1972.

Eisenberg, Abne and Ralph Smith. *Nonverbal Communication*. Indianapolis, Indiana: Bobbs-Merrill, 1971.

Ekman, Paul. *Darwin and Facial Expression: A Century of Research in Review*. New York: Academic Press, 1973.

Ekman, Paul, ed. *Expressions of Emotions in Man and Animals: Charles Darwin Centennial Volume*. New York: Academic Press, 1973.

Ekman, Paul. *Face of Man: Expressions of Universal Emtoions in a New Guinea Village*. New York: Garland STMP Press, 1980.

Ekman, Paul. *Telling Lies: Clues to Deceit in the Marketplace, Politics, and Marriage*. New York: Norton, 1985.

Ekman, Paul and Wallace V. Friesen. *Unmasking the Face: A Guide to Recognizing Emotions from Facial Cues*. Englewood Cliffs, New Jersey: Prentice-Hall, 1975.

Ekman, Paul and Wallace V. Friesen. *The Facial Action Coding System*. Palo Alto, California: Consulting Psychologists Press, 1978.

Ekman, Paul, W. Friesen, and P. Ellsworth. *Emotion in the Human Face: Guidelines for Research and an Integration of Findings*. New York: Pergamon, 1972.

Esser, A. H. *Use of Space by Animals and Men*. Bloomington: Indiana University Press, 1969.

Fast, Julius. *Body Language*. New York: Evans, 1970.

Feldman, Sandor S. *Mannerisms of Speech and Gesture in Everyday Life*. New York: International Universities Press, 1959.

Freedman, Jonathan L. *Crowding and Behavior*. San Francisco, California: W. H. Freeman, 1975.

Frye, Jerry K. *Frye's Index to Nonverbal Data*. Duluth: University of Minnesota Computer Center, 1980.

Fussell, Paul. *Class: A Guide through the American Status System*. New York: Summit, 1983.

Gittleson, Bernard. *Biorhythm: A Personal Science*. New York: Arco, 1975.

Goffman, Erving. *Behavior in Public Places*. New York: Free Press, 1963.

Gutman, Robert. *People and Buildings*. New York: Basic Books, 1972.

Harrison, Randall. *Beyond Words: An Introduction to Nonverbal Communication*. Englewood Cliffs, New Jersey: Prentice-Hall, 1974.

Hall, Edward T. *The Silent Language*. New York: Fawcett, 1959.

Hall, Edward T. *The Hidden Dimension*. Garden City, New York: Doubleday, 1966.

Henley, Nancy M. *Body Politics: Power, Sex, and Nonverbal Communication*. Englewood Cliffs, New Jersey: Prentice-Hall (Spectrum), 1977.

Hess, Ekhard. *The Tell-Tale Eye*. New York: Van Nostrand, 1975.

Hickson, Mark L. and Don W. Stacks. *NVC: Nonverbal Communication: Studies and Applications*. Dubuque, Iowa: Brown, 1985.

Hinde, Robert A. *Non-Verbal Communication*. Cambridge: Cambridge University Press, 1972.

Izard, C. E. *Face of Emotion*. New York: Appleton-Century-Crofts, 1971.

Katz, Albert M. and Virginia T. Katz, eds. *Foundations of Nonverbal Communication: Readings, Exercises, and Commentary*. Carbondale: Southern Illinois University Press, 1983.

Key, Mary R. *Paralanguage and Kinesics*. Metuchen, New Jersey: Scarecrow Press, 1975.

Keyes, Ralph. *The Height of Your Life*. New York: Warner Books, 1980.

Knapp, Mark L. *Nonverbal Communication in Human Interaction*, 2nd ed. New York: Holt, Rinehart and Winston, 1978.

Koneya, Mele and Alton Barbour. *Louder than Words: Nonverbal Communication*. Columbus, Ohio: Charles E. Merrill, 1976.

Lamb, Warren. *Posture and Gesture*. London: Duckworth, 1965.

Lamb, Warren and Elizabeth Watson. *Body Code: The Meaning in Movement*. Princeton, New Jersey: Princeton Book Co., 1987.

LaRusso, Dominic A. *The Shadows of Communication: Nonverbal Dimensions*. Dubuque, Iowa: Kendall/Hunt, 1977.

Leathers, Dale. *Nonverbal Communication Systems*. Boston: Allyn & Bacon, 1976.

Leathers, Dale. *Successful Nonverbal Communication: Principles and Applications*. New York: Macmillan, 1986.

Luce, Gay Gaer. *Body Time: Physiological Rhythms and Social Stress*. New York: Pantheon, 1971.

Lurie, Alison. *The Language of Clothes*. New York: Random House (Vintage), 1981.

Luscher, Max. *The Luscher Color Test*, trans. and ed., Ian A. Scott. New York: Pocket Books, 1969.

Malandro, Loretta, Larry Barker, and Deborah Ann Barker. *Nonverbal Communication*, 2nd ed. New York: Random House, 1988.

Mallardi, Vincent. *Biorhythms and Your Behavior*, rev ed. Philadelphia, Pennsylvania: Running Press, 1978.

Marshall, Evan. *Eye Language: Understanding the Eloquent Eye*. New York: New Trend, 1983.

Mehrabian, Albert. *Nonverbal Communication*. Chicago: Aldine-Atherton, 1972.

Mehrabian, Albert. *Silent Messages: Implicit Communication of Emotions and Attitudes*, 2nd ed. Belmont, California: Wadsworth, 1981.

Mehrabian, Albert. *Public Places and Private Spaces: The Psychology of Work, Play, and Living Environments*. New York: Basic Books, 1976.

Meerloo, Joost A. M. *Unobtrusive Communication*. Assen, Netherlands: Van Gorcum, 1964.

Molloy, John T. *Molloy's Live for Success*. New York: Bantam, 1981.

Montagu, Ashley. *Touching: The Human Significance of the Skin*. New York: Harper & Row, 1978.

Morris, Desmond. *Intimate Behaviour*. New York: Bantam, 1972.

Morris, Desmond. *Manwatching: A Field-Guide to Human Behavior*. New York: Abrams, 1977.

Morris, Desmond, Peter Collett, Peter Marsh, and Marie O'Shaughnessy. *Gestures: Their Origins and Distribution*. New York: Stein and Day, 1979.

Newman, Oscar. *Defensible Space*. New York: Collier, 1973.

Nierenberg, Gerard I. and Henry H. Calero. *How to Read a Person Like a Book*. New York: Pocket Books, 1971.

O'Neil, Barbara and Richard Phillips. *Biorhythms: How to Live with Your Life Cycles*. Pasadena, California: Ward Ritchie Press, 1975.

Pease, Allan. *Signals*. New York: Bantam, 1984.

Penry, Jacques. *How to Judge Character from the Face*. London: Hutchinson, 1939.

Pittinger, Robert E., Charles F. Hockett, and John J. Danehy. *The First Five Minutes*. Ithaca, New York: Paul Martineau, 1960.

Plaffman, Carl, ed. *Olfaction and Taste: Proceedings of the Third International Symposium*. New York: Rockefeller University Press, 986.

Polhemus, Ted, ed. *The Body Reader: Social Aspects of the Human Body*. New York: Pantheon Books, 1978.

Richmond, Virginia P., James McCroskey, and Steven K. Payne. *Nonverbal Behavior in Interpersonal Relations*. Englewood Cliffs, NJ: Prentice-Hall, 1987.

Rosenfeld, Lawrence and Jean Civikly. *With Words Unspoken*. New York: Holt, Rinehart and Winston, 1976.

Rosenthal, R. and L. Jacobsen. *Pygmalion in the Classroom*. New York: Holt, Rinehart and Winston, 1968.

Ruesch, Jurgen and W. Kees. *Nonverbal Communication: Notes on the Visual Perception of Human Relations*. Berkeley: University of California Press, 1956.

Saltus, Carol. *Body Scopes*. New York: Bantam, 1986.

Scheflen, Albert. *How Behavior Means*. New York: Gordon and Breach, 1974.

Scheflen, Albert and A. Scheflen. *Body Language and the Social Order.* Englewood Cliffs, New Jersey: Prentice-Hall (Spectrum), 1972.

Scherer, Klaus R. and Paul Ekman, eds. *Handbook of Methods in Nonverbal Behavior Research.* New York: Cambridge University Press, 1982.

Sebeok, Thomas A. *Semiotics: A Survey of the State of the Art.* The Hague: Mouton, 1972.

Sebeok, Thomas A., A. S. Hayes, and M. C. Bateson, eds. *Approaches to Semiotics.* The Hague: Mouton, 1964.

Siegman, A. W. and S. Feldstein, eds. *Multichannel Integration of Nonverbal Behavior.* Hillsdale, New Jersey: Lawrence Erlbaum, 1985.

Sommer, Robert. *Design Awareness.* San Francisco: Rinehart Press, 1972.

Sommer, Robert. *Personal Space: The Behavioral Basis of Design.* Englewood Cliffs, New Jersey: Prentice-Hall (Spectrum), 1969.

Spiegel, John and Povel Machotka. *Messages of the Body.* New York: Free Press, 1974.

Thompson, James J. *Beyond Words: Nonverbal Communication in the Classroom.* New York: Citation Press, 1973.

Watson, O. Michael. *Proxemic Behavior: A Cross-Cultural Study.* the Hague: Mouton, 1970.

Weimann, John and Randall Harrison, eds. *Nonverbal Communication: The Social Interaction Sphere.* Beverly Hills, California: Sage, 1983.

Weitz, Shirley, ed. *Nonverbal Communication: Readings with Commentary,* 2nd ed. New York: Oxford University Press, 1979.

Wiener, Morton and Albert Mehrabian. *Language within Language: Immediacy, a Channel in Nonverbal Communication.* New York: Appleton-Century-Crofts, 1968.

Winter, Ruth. *The Smell Book: Scents, Sex, and Society.* New York: Lippincott, 1976.

# Articles

Abercrombie, David. "Paralanguage," *British Journal of Disorders Communication* 3 (1968): 55-59.

Altman, I. "Privacy: A Conceptual Analysis," *Environment and Behavior* 8 (1976): 7-29.

Andersen, Peter A. and K. Leibowitz. "The Development and Nature of the Construct Touch Avoidance," *Environmental Psychology and Nonverbal Behavior* 3 (1978): 89-106.

Andrew, R. J. "The Origins of Facial Expression," *Scientific American* 213 (1965): 88-94.

Argyle, Michael and J. Dean. "Eye Contact, Distance and Affiliation," *Sociometry* 28 (1965): 289-304.

Argyle, Michael and R. Ingham. "Gaze, Mutual Gaze and Proximity," *Semiotica* 6 (1972): 32-49.

Barnlund, D. C. "Communicative Styles of Two Cultures: Public and Private Self in Japan and the United States," *Organization of Behavior in Face-to-Face Interaction*, ed. A. Kendon, R. M. Harris, and M. R. Key. The Hague: Mouton, 1975.

Berscheid, E., E. Walster, and G. Bohrnstedt. "Body Image: The Happy American Body," *Psychology Today* 7 (1973): 119-123, 126-131.

Boucher, J. D. and P. Ekman. "Facial Areas and Emotional Information," *Journal of Communication* 25 (1975): 21-29.

Bruneau, Thomas. "Communicative Silences: Forms and Functions," *Journal of Communication* 23 (1973): 17-46.

Bruneau, Thomas. "The Time Dimension in Intercultural Communication," in Larry A. Samovar and Richard E. Porter, eds., *Intercultural Communication: A Reader*, 4th ed. Belmont, California: Wadsworth, 1985, pp. 280-289.

Burgoon, Judee. "Nonverbal Communication Research in the 1970s: An Overview," *Communication Yearbook* 4, ed. D. Nimmo. New Brunswick, New Jersey: Transaction Books, 1980, pp. 179-197.

Burgoon, Judee. "Nonverbal Signals," *Handbook of Interpersonal Communication*, ed. Mark L. Knapp and Gerald R. Miller. Beverly Hills, California: Sage, 1985, pp. 344-390.

Cain, W. S. "To Know With the Nose: Keys to Odor Identification," *Science* 203 (1979):467-470.

Cain, W. S. "Educating Your Nose," *Psychology Today* (July 1981)

Cohen, A. A. "The Communicative Functions of Hand Illustrators," *Journal of Communication* 27 (1977): 54-63.

Cortes, J. B. and F. M. Gatti. "Physique and Self-description of Temperament," *Journal of Consulting Psychology* 29 (1965): 432-439.

Cuceloglu, D. M. "Perception of Facial Expressions in Three Different Cultures," *Ergonomics* 13 (1970): 93-100.

Duncan, S. D. "Some Signals and Rules for Taking Speaking Turns in Conversations," *Journal of Personality and Social Psychology* 23 (1972): 283-292.

Duncan, S. D. "On the Structure of Speaker-Auditor Interaction during Speaking Turns," *Language in Society* 2 (1974): 161-180.

Edney, J. J. "Human Territories: Comment on Functional Properties," *Environment and Behavior* 8 (1976): 31-47.

Ekman, Paul. "Universals and Cultural Differences in Facial Expressions of Emotions," *Nebraska Symposium on Motivation*, ed. J. Cole. Lincoln: University of Nebraska Press, 1972, pp. 207-283.

Ekman, Paul and W. V. Friesen. "Nonverbal Leakage and Clues to Deception," *Psychiatry* 32 (1969): 88-106.

Ekman, Paul and W. V. Friesen. "The Repertoire of Nonverbal Behavior: Categories, Origins, Usage, and Coding," *Semiotica* 1 (1969): 49-98.

Ekman, Paul and W. V. Friesen. "Hand Movements," *Journal of Communication* 22 (1972): 353-374.

Ekman, Paul and W. V. Friesen. "Detecting Deception from the Body or Face," *Journal of Personality and Social Psychology* 29 (1974): 288-298.

Ekman, Paul and W. V. Friesen. "Measuring Facial Movement," *Environmental Psychology and Nonverbal Behavior* 1 (1976): 56-75.

Ekman, Paul, W. V. Friesen, and S. S. Tomkins. "Facial Affect Scoring Technique: A First Validity Study," *Semiotica* 3 (1971): 37-58.

Feldman, Michael and Stephen Thayer. "A Comparison of Three Measures of Nonverbal Decoding Ability,"
*Journal of Social Psychology* 112 (1980): 91-97.

Friesen, Wallace V., Paul Ekman, and Harald Wallbott. "Measuring Hand Movements," *Journal of Nonverbal Behavior* 4 (1979): 97-112.

Haggard, E. A. and K. S. Isaacs. "Micromomentary Facial Expressions as Indicators of Ego Mechanisms in Psychotherapy," *Methods of Research in Psychotherapy*, ed., L. A. Gottschalk and A. H. Auerback. Englewood Cliffs, New Jersey: Prentice-Hall, 1966.

Hall, Edward T. "A System for the Notation of Proxemic Behavior," *American Anthropologist* 65 (1963): 1003-1026.

Hall, Edward T. "Proxemics," *Current Anthropology* 9 (1968): 83-108.

Hess, E. H. "Attitude and Pupil Size," *Scientific American* 212 (1965): 46-54.

Johnson, H. G., Paul Ekman, and W. V. Friesen. "Communicative Body Movements: American Emblems," *Semiotica* 15 (1975): 335-353.

Jones, Stanley E. "Sex Differences in Touch Communication," *Western Journal of Speech Communication* 50 (1986): 227-241.

Jones, Stanley E. and A. Elaine Yarbrough. "A Naturalistic Study of the Meanings of Touch," *Communication Monographs* 52 (1985): 19-56.

Jourard, Sidney M. "An Exploratory Study of Body-Accessibility," *British Journal of Social and Clinical Psychology* 5 (1966): 221-231.

Jourard, Sidney M. and J. E. Rubin. "Self-Disclosure and Touching: A Study of Two Models of Interpersonal Encounter and their Interrelation," *Journal of Humanistic Psychology*, 8 (1968): 39-48.

Jourard, Sidney M. and P. F. Secord. "Body-Cathexis and Personality," *British Journal of Psychology* 46 (1955): 130-138.

Keith, L. Thomas, Louis G. Tornatsky, and L. Pettigrew. "An Analysis of Verbal and Nonverbal Classroom Teaching Behaviors," *Journal of Experimental Education* 42 (1974): 30-38.

Kleinke, Chris L. and Frederick B. Meeker. "Effects of Gaze, Touch, and Use of Name on Evaluation of Engaged Couples," *Journal of Research in Personality* 7 (1974): 368-373.

Knapp, Mark L. "The Study of Nonverbal Behaviour Vis-a-vis Human Communication Theory," in *Nonverbal Behaviour: Perspectives, Applications, Intercultural Insights*, ed. A. Wolfgang. New York: C. J. Hogrefe, Inc., 1984.

Knapp, Mark L., Michael J. Cody, and Kathleen Kelley Reardon. "Nonverbal Signals," in *Handbook of Communication Science*, ed., Charles R. Berger and Steven H. Chaffee. Beverly Hills, California: Sage, 1987, pp. 385-418.

Knapp, Mark L., R. P. Hart, G. W. Friedrich, and G. M. Shulman. "The Rhetoric of Goodbye: Verbal and Nonverbal Correlates of Human Leave-Taking," *Communication Monographs* 40 (1973): 182-198.

Knapp, Mark L., J. M. Wiemann, and J. A. Daly. "Nonverbal Communication: Issues and Appraisal," *Human Communication Research* 4 (1978): 271-279.

Knight, David J., Daniel Langmeyer, and David C. Lundgren. "Eye-Contact, Distance, and Affiliation: The Role of Observer Bias," *Sociometry* 36 (1973): 390-401.

Livingston, Samuel A. "Nonverbal Communication Tests as Predictors of Success in Psychology and Counseling," *Applied Psychological Measurement* 5 (1981): 325-331.

Lott, D. F. and Robert Sommer. "Seating Arrangements and Status," *Journal of Personality and Social Psychology* 7 (1967): 90-95.

Lyman, S. M. and M. B. Scott. "Territoriality: A Neglected Sociological Dimension," *Social Problems* 15 (1967): 236-249.

MacKay, D. M. "Formal Analysis of Communication Processes," in *Nonverbal Communication,* ed., R. A. Hinde. Cambridge: Cambridge University Press, 1972.

Maclay, Howard and Charles E. Osgood. "Hesitation Phenomena in Spontaneous English Speech," *Word* 15 (1959): 19-44.

Murray, Robert P. and Hugh McGinley. "Looking as a Measure of Attraction," *Journal of Applied Social Psychology* 2 (1972): 267-274.

Newman, Helen. "The Sounds of Silence in Communicative Encounters," *Communication Quarterly* 30 (1982): 142-149.

Nguyen, M. L. R. Heslin, and M. L. Nguyen. "Meanings of Touch: Sex Differences," *Journal of Communication* 25 (1975): 92-103.

Porter, R. H. and J. D. Moore. "Human Kin Recognition by Olfactory Cues," *Physiology and Behavior* 27 (1981):493-495.

Rosenfeld, L. B., S. Kartus, and C. Ray. "Body Accessibility Revisited," *Journal of Communication* 26 (1976): 27-30.

Rosenfeld, L. B. and T. G. Plax. "Clothing as Communication," *Journal of Communication* 27 (1977): 24-31.

Rozelle, Richard M., Daniel Druckman, and James C. Baxter. "Nonverbal Communication," in *A Handbook of Communication Skills,* ed., Owen Hargie. New York: New York University Press, 1986, pp. 59-94.

Sainsbury, Peter and Elizabeth Wood. "Measuring Gesture: Its Cultural and Clinical Correlates," *Psychological Medicine* 7 (1977): 63-72.

Scheflen, Albert E. "The Significance of Posture in Communication Systems," *Psychiatry* 27 (1964): 316-331.

Scheflen, Albert E. "Quasi-Courtship Behavior in Psychotherapy," *Psychiatry* 28 (1965): 245-257.

Schleidt, M. "Personal Odor and Nonverbal Communication," *Ethology and Sociobiology* 1 (1980):225-231.

Shadish, William R. "Nonverbal Interventions in Clinical Groups," *Journal of Consulting and Clinical Psychology* 48 (1980): 164-168.

Sommer, Robert. "Studies in Personal Space," *Sociometry* 22 (1959): 247-260.

Sommer, Robert. "Further Studies in Small Group Ecology," *Sociometry* 28 (1965): 337-348.

Sommer, Robert. "Man's Proxemic Environment," *Journal of Social Issues* 22 (1966): 59-70.

Thakerar, J. and H. Giles. "They Are—So They Spoke" Noncontent Speech Stereotypes," *Language and Communication* 1 (1981): 255-261.

Trager, G. L. "Paralangauge: A First Approximation," *Studies in Linguistics* 13 (1958): 1-12.

Trager, G. L. "The Typology of Paralanguage," *Anthropological Linguistics* 3 (1961): 17-21.

Trzcinka, Gary P. "The Reliability of Measuring Nonverbal Behavior Accompanying Speech," *Biological Psychology Bulletin* 5 (1977): 29-37.

Wallbott, Harald G. "Hand Movement Quality: A Neglected Aspect of Nonverbal Behavior in Cinical Judgment and Person Perception," *Journal of Clinical Psychology* 41 (1985): 345-359.

Wiemann, J. M. and M. L. Knapp. "Turn-Taking in Conversations," *Journal of Communication* 25 (1975): 75-92.

Zuckerman, M., J. A. Hall, R. S. Defrank, and R. Rosenthal. "Encoding and Decoding of Spontaneous and Posed Facial Expressions," *Journal of Personality and Social Psychology* 34 (1977): 966-977.

Zuckerman, M., M. S. Lipets, and J. H. Koivumaki. "Encoding and Decoding Nonverbal Cues of Emotion," *Journal of Personality and Social Psychology* 32 (1975): 1068-1076.